ZERO PROOF COCKTAILS

ZERO PROOF COCKTAILS

90 Non-Alcoholic Recipes for Mindful Drinking

ELVA RAMIREZ

PHOTOGRAPHY BY
ROBERT BREDVAD

HOUGHTON MIFFLIN HARCOURT
BOSTON NEW YORK 2021

For information about permission to reproduce selections from
this book, write to trade.permissions@hmhco.com or to
Permissions, Houghton Mifflin Harcourt Publishing Company,
3 Park Avenue, 19th Floor, New York, New York 10016.

hmhbooks.com

Library of Congress Cataloging-in-Publication Data
Names: Ramirez, Elva, author.
Title: Zero proof cocktails : 90 non-alcoholic recipes for mindful drinking /
Elva Ramirez ; photography by Robert Bredvad.
Description: Boston : Houghton Mifflin Harcourt, [2021] | Includes bibliographical references and index.
Identifiers: LCCN 2020039131 (print) | LCCN 2020039132 (ebook)
ISBN 9780358211914 (hardback) | ISBN 9780358213468 (ebook)
Subjects: LCSH: Cocktails. | Non-alcoholic beverages. | LCGFT: Cookbooks.
Classification: LCC TX951 .R152 2021 (print) | LCC TX951 (ebook) | DDC 641.87/4—dc23
LC record available at https://lccn.loc.gov/2020039131
LC ebook record available at https://lccn.loc.gov/2020039132

ISBN 978-0-358-21191-4 (pob)
ISBN 978-0-358-21346-8 (ebk)

Book design by Claudia Wu

Printed in China
SCP 10 9 8 7 6 5 4 3 2 1

CONTENTS

ACKNOWLEDGMENTS

Thank you, Team Zero Proof.

First round of gratitude goes to my agent, Leigh Eisenman, and my editor, Justin Schwartz, for believing in me and this project from the start. It all starts here.

Thank you, Susan Choung, for your sharp eyes, hard work, and patience in recipe editing.

Thank you, Abeo Miller, my lovely recipe-testing partner, for invaluable bartending help and for taking on extra-long workdays so we could spend several hours making drinks. Thank you, Masa Urushido, for kindly letting us use Katana Kitten's bar for drinks testing.

Thank you, Robert Bredvad, Maeve Sheridan, and Mallory Lance, for your unflagging enthusiasm in bringing this project to life with your unmatched visual skills.

Thank you, Ben Branson and Lorena Tapiero. Your crucial insights into the developing no-proof space and your dedication to drinking better are the cornerstones of this emerging category and lifestyle.

Thank you, Charles Gibb and Amanda Stackman. Few people can pivot from silly martinis to no-proof drinks in a single conversation—and identify global drinking trends as they emerge.

Thank you to my circle of BFFs. Jenna Gerbino Kaplan, Mark Silver, Madeleine Andrews, and Helen Zhang, you are always around to offer support and listen to rants, no matter the time of night or the messaging platform.

Thank you, Phil Pearson. You listen like a best friend and give advice like a CEO. This would have turned out much differently if it weren't for you.

Thank you, Robert Gerard Pietrusko, Will Davis, and Jason Velasquez. A girl always needs someone to count on; thanks for being there, no questions asked.

Thank you to every bartender who contributed recipes to this project. I couldn't have done this without you. You are all stars.

Thank you to everyone I interviewed for this book. The first interview took place in the East Village in March 2019. I interviewed experts in New York, London, Paris, Mexico City, Chicago, Minneapolis, Las Vegas, Glasgow, Rotterdam, and Los Angeles before it was all over.

Lastly, thank you, Tyler, the Creator. I'm not going to front like I know you. But your entire discography formed the soundtrack to a year's worth of hard work, and your boundless creative energy is contagious.

INTRODUCTION
A New Era of No-Proof Drinking

It's been nearly one hundred years since Prohibition was repealed, but the biggest trend in cocktails has nothing to do with alcohol.

Non-alcoholic drinks first came to my mind in August 2013, when I wrote about "summer mocktails" in the *Wall Street Journal*. The short piece, which featured no-proof recipes as well as their boozy adaptations, noted that "the alcohol-free cocktail is cropping up everywhere around town." And while that was true, it would be several more years before the non-alcoholic drink would be taken seriously, in New York City and elsewhere. I recall it took some effort to find a few no-proof drinks, and on the advice of an editor we profiled a fresh juice venue that wasn't properly a bar but that did serve inventive drinks.

As late as 2013, we were still calling these drinks "mocktails," as the *WSJ* headline says. Later, as the zero-proof drink gained the attention of the bar community, its terminology, as well as composition, was given serious reconsideration.

There was a turning point for bars in 2015. That was the year Seedlip, the first non-alcoholic distillate, launched in London, where it not only sold out its inaugural Selfridges run, but found itself embraced by London's top bars, including American Bar at The Savoy Hotel. Seedlip's smashing debut turned heads at spirits behemoth Diageo, which bought a minority stake in the fledgling brand just a year after its launch. That marked the first time that Diageo, through their accelerator, Distill Ventures, invested in a non-alcoholic company. By the time Diageo acquired a majority stake in Seedlip a few years later, the brand had grown to encompass two product lines, six expressions, and over 10,000 global accounts.

When Seedlip arrived stateside, it inspired American bartenders to begin toying around with the mixer; more non-alcoholic drink options, Seedlip or otherwise, began edging onto menus at places like Manhattan's The Fat Radish.

"I think it is here to stay," Brian Evans, head bartender at Sunday in Brooklyn, said of the emerging movement. "One of the biggest trends in cocktails last year was zero proof. It took us all by storm."

In July 2018, at the Tales of the Cocktail spirits conference, William Grant & Sons, which owns Reyka vodka, Hendrick's Gin, and Glenfiddich, among other spirits brands, took an unprecedented step to throw its first fully non-alcoholic party. The conference, held every July in New Orleans, is famous for splashy portfolio parties, in which brands such as Bacardi, Pernod Ricard, and others spend hundreds of thousands of dollars on all-you-can-drink bacchanalias. For William Grant & Sons, hosting a fully dry event was a significant gesture that nodded toward the conversation about wellness in the bar world and the growing sophistication of no-proof cocktails. It was also a tacit acknowledgment that the liquor industry need not be threatened by the rise in boozeless drinks.

It's not just spirits companies who are now pivoting toward the spirit-free space.

Anheuser-Busch, the largest beer brewer in the world, has a global portfolio of more than 500 brands, including multiple non-alcoholic and low-alcoholic brands, such as Budweiser Prohibition Brew and Golden Road's Mango Cart wheat ale. With an eye on emerging drink trends, the company, known as AB InBev, now has a dedicated executive position, the chief non-alcohol beverages officer, tasked with the specific mission of cultivating the non-drinking consumer. In recent years, non-alcoholic sales at AB InBev grew to around 10 percent of global beer volumes. As part of its Global Smart Drinking Goals initiative, AB InBev aims to raise its low- and non-alcoholic sales to 20 percent of global beer volume[1] by the end of 2025. AB InBev rival Carlsberg, meanwhile, has seen non-alcoholic sales[2] in Western Europe jump sharply, and Heineken's first non-alcoholic beer, Heineken 0.0, found a warm reception when it debuted across Europe and the United States.

Even amid new product launches, media coverage, and customer requests, though, you'll find pockets of skepticism about boozeless drinks, in the same way traditional restaurants once scoffed at requests for vegetarian or gluten-free dishes. But as some of the world's most respected bartenders and bars give the no-proof drink the same attention as boozy concoctions, crafting high-end no-ABV cocktails is emerging as the bar world's newest challenge. ("ABV" is short for "alcohol by volume," which is another way of designating "proof," or the percentage of alcohol something contains.) As in the worlds of fashion and music, when top industry names take something seriously, their peers take note.

For bars, offering zero-proof drinks on their menus (or not) is an economic decision. It makes good business sense for restaurants and bars to elevate their non-alcoholic drinks: They can show off their skills and charge more for a drink that represents their ethos in a way that a mere soda water doesn't. Even bars that don't officially offer non-alcoholic drinks on menus will often concede that they can whip up zero-proof drinks on demand.

Hospitality professionals know that regular drinkers (even bartenders) will sometimes choose to take a night (or a month) off from alcohol. The no-proof drinker is no longer someone who eschews alcohol for sober living or due to pregnancy or illness; zero proof appeals to the full spectrum of contemporary drinkers, including those who still partake.

More bars, such as the various properties in the SoHo House portfolio, making their own flavored tonics and seltzers, which bring depth and complexity to virgin drinks. Additionally, as the craft cocktail movement enters its second decade, there's more knowledge (and experts) than ever when it comes to elevated techniques, sourcing, and drink styles. It was only a matter of time before the no-proof drink became the new focus of experimentation for cocktail professionals.

Some entrepreneurs go all in on no-proof drinks. In October 2018, Listen Bar, a fully non-alcoholic bar, debuted as a five-day pop-up in Williamsburg, Brooklyn, before moving into a monthly residency at Von, a bar in Lower Manhattan. Listen Bar's charismatic founder, Lorelei Bandrovschi, quickly became the face of the growing no-proof movement, illustrating that non-drinking is not only a valid choice, but can be a youthful and exuberant stance as well.

Listen Bar might seem like it would be a bar outlier, but it has several peers, including Brooklyn's Getaway, Pittsburgh's Empath, Austin's Sans Bar, and Dublin's Virgin Mary Bar. At the start of 2020, Wildcrafters opened its doors in Jacksonville, Florida, and two no-proof spaces debuted in London, including a concept space from beer distiller BrewDog.

Sober bars tap into a wave of cultural forces making the dry cocktail not just cool but desirable. The start of the new year, for example, rings in Dry January, a month of sober drinking and detoxing after a holiday season of indulgence.

Dry January is a monthlong abstinence initiative from Alcohol Change UK, an alcohol-awareness non-profit. Around 4,000 people signed up for the first official campaign in 2012. By 2018, over 4 million people in the U.K. alone said they were abstaining, up 35 percent from the previous year.[3] By 2020, one in ten Britons said they were giving up drinking at the start of the year.

But Dry January is representative of a bigger overall trend for millennials, one that suggests that some people think about abstaining for longer than just one month.

In 2017, 20 percent (or 10.4 million) of adult Britons described themselves as teetotalers, or those who never drink alcohol. By gender, that breaks down to 22.6 percent of British women and 18.1 percent of British men. This is part of a trend tracked by Britain's Office for National Statistics, which has found that since 2005, teetotalism has increased[4] among ages 16 to 44. In 2015, 29 percent of British students (ages 16 to 24) reported they were teetotalers.[5] According to the study's lead researcher, the rise in sober young people occurred across a full range of demographics, suggesting that non-drinking is becoming more mainstream, and even cool, among swaths of youths (while conversely, being drunk is seen as tacky and outdated).

Even as the chatter around non-drinking grows, for consumers it can still be difficult to abstain from drinking, or to always find viable options that aren't just fizzy waters. When I was about two months out from my deadline to turn in this book, I decided I would stop drinking until the entire manuscript was written.

Easier said than done. I got caught up in New Year's Eve celebrations and suffered a New Year's Day hangover that was memorable for its levels of pain and discomfort. In many ways, that's not an accident, because drinking while socializing is deeply ingrained in our culture, even as nearly every drinker can describe at least one vicious hangover in great detail. No one is surprised when they get sick from drinking too much, yet many of us will sign up for another night of carousing once the pain eases.

It's difficult, but not impossible, to go out and not be tempted by liquor. Even as the zero-proof movement gets bigger, there are many bars that don't offer no-proof options, and instead put the burden on the consumer. That's part of our cultural makeup in the U.S. This book will examine American drinking culture and the pressure to drink all the time, which might feel modern but actually dates back to the founding of the American colonies.

As the success of Listen Bar shows, the rise of the no-proof movement is an opportunity to examine how we socialize and how we speak about socializing, as well as how we drink. It's time to rechristen the spirit-free drink as brainy but not dull, lively but not intoxicating, sophisticated but not overwrought, as desirable but not embarrassing. As the craft no-ABV drink grows up, so does the audience for it. Today, the no-proof drinker is really anyone.

We all know what the most talented bartenders in the world can do with spirits. What happens when they are challenged to make exceptional drinks, but without booze? This book answers that question.

This is the start of the new era for zero-proof drinking.

THE ZERO-PROOF GUIDE TO AT-HOME DRINKS

From proper barware to tips on reducing waste, here's your primer on what you'll need before whipping up a round of cocktails.

TIPS ON TECHNIQUE AND PRODUCTS

Learn to think like a bartender. Great drinks don't start when you pour liquid into a tin; they come to life during the prep stage. What happens during prep impacts your finished drink.

It's easy to lose track of what you're doing, especially when making a new recipe for the first time. Set up what bartenders call *mise en place*. That means working in a clean, uncluttered space, where all your tools and prepped ingredients are laid out neatly in front of you, and putting everything back in its place when you're done with it. This will avoid unnecessary hunting for things and distractions.

Use the freshest and highest-quality items you can buy. A bad fruit will yield bad juice. If you wouldn't eat it, it's probably not a good idea to juice it.

Always use high-quality tonics and soda waters. Mixers from brands such as Fever-Tree, London Essence Co., and Q Mixers are strongly suggested over supermarket brands, which have higher sugar content in their tonics and less minerality in their club sodas. A bad mixer will drown out the delicate flavors of the syrups you just spent time making.

If the recipe calls for fruit peels, organic produce is best.

If you peel fruits, such as apples, before juicing, the juice will have less sediment and color. Alternatively, you can pour fresh fruit

juice through a coffee filter to remove pulp and color.

Unless a recipe calls for you to pour a drink or ingredient into a glass, always strain into a glass filled with fresh ice. It's just prettier.

Strain away all solids in syrups; small bits of organic material will eventually turn the mixture bitter.

Let all syrups fully cool before covering them. Placing a lid on a still-warm syrup provides an opportunity for the growth of bacteria, which are attracted to warmth and sugars.

Always label and date your syrups and juices. It's very easy to lose track of when you made something.

Extend the life of your syrups by breaking them up into two or more containers and freezing what you don't need. Once you've defrosted the syrup, don't freeze it again.

Kalustyan's in New York City is the best place to pick up rare ingredients you won't find at the local grocery store. They have competitive prices and the best selection this side of Amazon, plus they take online orders. Find them at foodsofnations.com.

Garnishes, as any cocktail enthusiast knows, add that extra-special touch. If you're throwing a party or want to impress your guests, invest in fresh, colorful garnishes such as edible flowers or colorful herbs. You'll always find a great seasonal selection at Chef's Garden (chefs-garden.com), a small family farm that serves the best restaurants in the U.S.

Can't find an ingredient on Amazon? Try Etsy, which is emerging as an alternative marketplace for rare products from small businesses.

If space permits, keep your glassware in the freezer so it's chilled when you pour a drink into it.

Need to make crushed ice? You can wrap loose ice cubes in a clean dish towel or muslin bag and break them up with a kitchen mallet or metal tin. You can also buy reusable kits on Amazon.

REDUCING WASTE AND USING LEFTOVER INGREDIENTS

Learn to think like a bartender, part two. The bar world doesn't stop working once a drink is served; bartenders often look for ways to use leftover products rather than tossing anything. Seek to reduce waste, every single time you make a drink.

Have a lot of extra citrus peels? Old citrus juice? Look up some of the cordial recipes in this book, where you combine peels and/or juice with water and sugar. Cordials are very adaptable and easy to make.

You will likely end up with extra juices and teas, which all have a short lifespan. Store them separately, but then create spontaneous mixes each morning until you run out. Green teas are great for tempering the sour pucker of intense citrus. One of my favorite informal breakfast drinks includes calamansi, pineapple, and mango purees shaken up with chilled jasmine tea and a splash of honey syrup.

I always keep a bottle of high-quality Bloody Mary mix (such as from Stonewall Kitchen or Morris Kitchen) in the fridge. Whenever I have leftover savory juices, such as carrot or beet, I combine them in a mixing tin, add Bloody Mary mix, shake with ice, then top off with any of the vinegars or brines I have laying around. (Kombucha adds a nice touch as well.)

Savory vegetable juices, such as yellow bell pepper, mix well with sour citrus juices, like calamansi.

Mint tea or mint syrup brings a bright herbal dimension to savory and citrus juices.

Agave and honey syrups, especially the flavored variations in this book, pair well with sharp citrus juices. Also use them for topping yogurt.

Every flavored syrup in this book can be used in multiple ways. Natasha David's syrups, in particular the vanilla turmeric and sous vide chai syrups (pages 203 and 206, respectively), were an absolute revelation. I use a tablespoon or two of flavored syrup in my morning coffee or tea every day.

Invest in reusable metal straws for drinks that call for straws. Plus, they're more attractive than one-use plastic straws.

THE NO-PROOF BARTENDER'S TOOL KIT

Ready to shake up some no-proof drinks?
Before you start, here are a few things you'll want to have on hand.

GOOD BAR TOOLS. You'll need at least one mixing tin, a mixing glass, and jiggers. Cocktail Kingdom (cocktailkingdom.com), which is the favorite retailer for many bars, is the best place to start for bartender-approved gear, including glassware, strainers, and mixing spoons.

A GRAM SCALE. Most scales toggle between grams and ounces, which is helpful when you are measuring dry and wet ingredients. Try to get the most sensitive scale you can afford since some measurements, such as for acid powders, will be small.

THE BEST JUICER YOU CAN AFFORD. Many of these recipes use fresh juices, so it's a great idea to have one handy (plus, think of the healthy ways you can kick up your daily routine). I did a lot of research before picking up a Breville juicer, and I'm absolutely a fan. Breville is the juicer brand I see most often at bars, for what it's worth.

A GOOD FINE-MESH STRAINER. Nearly every drink and every syrup is strained at least once, while others are strained multiple times. Get a strainer, or two in different sizes, so that you can fit one over a jar or container and let mixes strain while you clean up.

A SOUS VIDE IMMERSION CIRCULATOR. Cooking sous vide means slow cooking foods in a sealed container in a hot water bath. This allows for controlled cooking that also seals in flavors. Amazon has a wide range of immersion circulators across multiple price points; invest in the best quality product you can afford. I chose a less expensive model and came to regret it.

HEAVY GLASS MASON JARS AND BOTTLES. In the interest of reducing waste, I prefer to use heat-proof glass jars, instead of one-use plastic sous vide bags, for cooking syrups. You'll also need glass bottles to store syrups in the fridge. Do not use glass for freezing, as the glass will crack when the frozen syrups expand.

PLASTIC CONTAINERS OR BOTTLES WITH LIDS. Reusable plastic containers are key for freezing syrups and juices.

REUSABLE FINE-MESH MUSLIN BAGS. For fine straining and clarifying, I prefer muslin bags, such as those used for making nut milks, to cheesecloth, which can only be used once.

BASIC KITCHEN TOOLS. You probably have measuring cups and measuring spoons but it's worth mentioning.

A BRIEF HISTORY OF TEMPERANCE

THE COLONIAL ERA
TO THE LATE NINETEENTH CENTURY

To be American is to drink. To be American is to worry about drinking.

The inclination to drink all day, at all times, and its countering impulse to regulate and control how much other people drink all day and at all times, is deeply woven into the American character. This tension, between seeing the enjoyment of alcohol as an intrinsic individual freedom and viewing liquor as a public health risk, predates America itself. European colonists arriving in the New World aimed to maintain their traditional drinking patterns even as they built settlements in their new adopted land. As what would become the United States evolved out of those early colonies, the public perception of alcohol, and its attendant anxieties, grew out of seeds first planted in the 1600s.

At the very start of America's colonial era, before there were cities and when there were only a handful of settlers in the New World, there was a brew house.

When the Pilgrims first arrived in what is now Massachusetts in November 1620, they were running low on everything from food to morale. The settlers had brought beer over on the *Mayflower*, but by December they were down to their last few barrels. What beer remained was jealously guarded by the *Mayflower's* captain, Christopher Jones, who needed to make sure he would have enough supplies for his crew when the *Mayflower* made its return voyage in the spring of 1621. Crew members were promised as much as a gallon of beer per day; along with keeping the sailors motivated, the daily intake of beer kept away signs of scurvy.[6]

A brew house was among the first buildings set up by the Pilgrims in Plymouth.[7] A tavern was built soon after. The inaugural Thanksgiving, held in the fall of 1621, featured beer made using the settlers' first barley crop.

The Plymouth colony was an improvement on the one in Jamestown, Virginia, established by 104 colonists in the spring of 1607. The Jamestown colonists, "lured to the New World by the promise of a sober lifestyle and a healthy diet,"[8] did not have anyone among them with brewing experience. When the ship that dropped off the Jamestown settlers returned to England on June 22, 1607, those left behind lamented that "there remained neither taverne, beere-house, nor place of relife but the common kettell." "Our drink was water, our lodgings, castles in the aire," settler Thomas Studley wrote.[9]

The lack of a brewery in Jamestown, among other things, would have dire consequences, because early settlers turned to drinking river water, which was tainted with microorganisms and had a high salt content. As a result, by January 1608, only 34 of the original 104 settlers were still (barely) alive.

In 1608, new settlers arrived in Jamestown, among them a perfumer, a jeweler, a tailor, a barber, and 119 "gentlemen," but there was still no one in the fledgling colony with the skills to make water potable. In 1609, with the colony still foundering, advertisements went out in England for two brewers. The search for brewing expertise, by that point, was a matter of public health.

Colonists died of "Swellings, Flixes and Burning Fevers," some suffered through "wild vomits into the black night."[11] At the time, as now, colonists were thought to have been brought low by waterborne diseases[12] or, as Virginia governor Francis Wyatt described it, "the intemperate drinking of water."

"To plant a Colony by water drinkers was an inexcusable error in those, who laid the first foundation," Governor Wyatt wrote in 1622.

According to geological historian Carville Earle, "At flood tide, colonists drank water containing salt in concentrations of over five parts per thousand—far above the recommended standard today for constant daily usage of one per thousand. The colonists suffered from salt poisoning, with its characteristic symptoms of 'swellings' (edema), lassitude, and irritability." The Jamestown colonists, despite setting up early trade with local Native Americans and the occasional gifts of food from friendly tribes, would eventually endure "The Starving Time," which historians have debated eventually led to cannibalism during the winter of 1609.[13]

The mistakes made in Jamestown weren't repeated in Plymouth. "Drinking water—any water—was a sign of desperation, an admission of abject poverty, a last resort," Frank Chapelle wrote in *Wellsprings*, a history of spring water. "Only truly poor people, who had absolutely no choice, drank water."[14] Although water was used for cooking, it was associated with what you gave livestock and it posed a real health risk.

By 1634, the British Crown required New England colonies to have a tavern. Before there were courthouses and city halls, the tavern was the center of colonial life. It was where neighbors gathered, where town business was handled, where new visitors were welcomed.

It was in the colonial tavern, established in the earliest days of the country, where distilled spirits took their prime place in American life. Along with rum and whiskey, early Americans drank cider, beer, wine, and applejack. Since this was well before the advent of refrigeration, milk could be hard to come by outside the home and was typically reserved for children. (Even milk could be sketchy; if cattle ate poisonous weeds, those toxins were passed on via their milk.)

A lack of many non-alcoholic options, amplified by a well-founded distrust of water, wove hard drinking into every facet of daily life, and imprinted a love of liquor into the DNA of American culture.

People, even children, drank in the morning before heading to work or school. There wasn't a coffee break during the colonial era but there was the "elevens," when gentlemen would pause their work for a pre-lunch tipple. Americans drank before dinner, during dinner, and then again after dinner.[15] "At trials the bottle was passed among spectators, attorneys, clients—and to the judge," W. J. Rorabaugh wrote in his excellent *The Alcoholic Republic*. "Alcohol was pervasive in American society; it crossed regional, sexual, racial, and class lines. Americans drank at home and abroad, alone and together, at work and at play, in fun and in earnest," Rorabaugh noted. "They drank from the crack of dawn to the crack of dawn." Colonial-era spirits (rum, whiskey, gin, and brandy), it should be noted, were about 90 proof (or 45 percent alcohol); lower-proof beverages such as beer (5 percent alcohol), cider (10 percent alcohol), and wine (18 percent alcohol) were, briefly, considered close to non-alcoholic (which is why the earliest temperance societies at first allowed their followers to drink beer, wine, and cider). "Small beer," sometimes made at home, was something like beer-flavored water and came in at 1 percent alcohol.[16]

Given the ubiquity of all-day drinking, it's no surprise that drunken behavior emerged as a problem. Town elders imposed closing times on taverns and punished disruptive drunks and the tavern owners who served them to excess. As Susan Cheever wrote in *Drinking in America*, the first drunk arrest in Plymouth took place in 1635: "The instigator was one John Holmes, who got so drunk that his punishment was time in the stocks and a twenty-shilling fine."[17]

Colonial liquor laws were necessary because early Americans drank, and they drank a lot. According to historian Iain Gately, "In 1810, federal statistics show that the six main whiskey-producing states together distilled twice as many gallons of whiskey per annum as there were people in America." Ten years later, "nine million women and children drank twelve million gallons, and three million men accounted for the other sixty million."[18]

Incidentally, the nineteenth century's liquor flush led to a new American art form. The first known reference to the word *cocktail* (first printed as "cock-tail," then "cock tail") in the U.S., according to Gately, was a newspaper mention in the May 6, 1806, issue of *The Balance, and Columbian Repository,* a New York–based newspaper, "which published the drinks bill of a political candidate." The paper's editor later explained to readers: "Cock tail, then, is a stimulating liquor, composed of a spirits of any kind, sugar, water, and bitters . . . [It] renders the heart stout and bold, at the same time that it fuddles the head."[19]

By the early 1700s, discomfort about public drunkenness evolved from individual dismay into a grassroots movement. The early temperance movement gained steam when Dr. Benjamin Rush, a signer of the Declaration of Independence, wrote several articles denouncing alcohol's effects. Rush's *An Inquiry Into the Effects of Spirituous Liquors* (1784) detailed, from a medical point of view, the various health impacts of drinking, which were just becoming recognized by the medical establishment. Due to his Revolutionary star cred, Rush's articles gained wide notice and were immediately popular. By 1850, Rush's works had been reprinted over 170,000 times.[20]

The temperance cause was helped when water got a long-overdue image upgrade in the late 1700s. Borrowing from the European custom of visiting hot springs for medicinal purposes, some post-Revolutionary-era entrepreneurs established hotels and inns around springs in New England. Naturally effervescent water,[21] such as that from Saratoga Springs, New York, became available for sale in bottles, for those who could afford it.

Philadelphia's Quakers so popularized the waters from Yellow Springs, Chester County, that a road, and later an inn, were built there in 1750. "By 1800, drinking water had entirely lost its association with poverty and was a sign of wealth and sophistication," Chapelle wrote in *Wellsprings.* (Cities, starting with Philadelphia, began getting piped water circa 1799. Anti-water fears still lingered, however, as people were warned not to drink water too quickly.)

A letter to the editor printed in the May 31, 1811, issue of Richmond, Virginia's *The Enquirer* extolled the virtues of Yellow Springs. "The obvious effects of this water, upon drinking it, are 1st, a sensible flushing of the face, or rather a pleasant warm glow is felt, attended with an increase in pulsations," the author, identified only as "Viator," wrote. "It is strongly diuretic, and is light upon the stomach, and instead of causing uneasiness, or depression in spirits, tho drank in considerable quantity, gives hilarity."[22]

According to an early history of the temperance movement published in 1881, one of the first temperance meetings, inspired by Rush's writings, took place in Litchfield, Connecticut, in July 1789. Over two hundred of "the most respectable farmers . . . have formed themselves into an association to discourage the use of spirituous liquors, and have determined not to use any kind of distilled liquors, in doing their farming work, the ensuing season." [23]

It's worth noting that at the start of the movement, "temperance" and "total abstinence" (or "teetotalism") referred to two different takes on drinking. "Temperance," when the term first emerged, referred to moderate, or mindful, drinking, and made allowances for wine, cider, and beer. (One historian notes that because of these exceptions, it wasn't uncommon to find some temperance society members drunk at their own meetings.) Eventually, many temperance societies ended up adopting a total abstinence stance against intoxicating liquors of all kinds.

The American Society for the Promotion of Temperance (established 1826) was unambiguous about its policy: "That in opposing the use of ardent spirits,no substitute, except pure water, be recommended as a drink."[24] In its 1836 annual report, the society claimed over 8,000 temperance societies across 23 states, totaling an estimated 1.5 million members. The society took credit for closing 4,000 distilleries and convincing over 8,000 merchants to give up selling liquor.

In a savvy move, long before contemporary corporations embraced the power of messaging through all forms of media, the temperance movement deployed a host of methods to reach potential new members.

Temperance societies started their own newspapers (such as Boston's *National Philanthropist*) and newsletters. Throughout the 1800s, pamphlets with titles such as "The temperance textbook: A collection of facts and interesting anecdotes illustrating the evils of intoxicating drinks" (1837) and "Anti-Bacchus: An essay on the evils connected with the use of intoxicating drinks" (1840) were published.

By the mid-1800s, the temperance movement acquired something it had previously lacked: political clout. The "drys," as they were known, found worthy rivals in "wet" brewers and the hospitality industry, who also learned to lobby politicians. In 1851, Maine was the first state to ban the sale of alcohol for personal use. Shortly after, Delaware, New York, Michigan, and Ohio, among others, enacted versions of the "Maine Law," some of which were struck down by courts, revised, then signed into law.

When the nation was divided by the Civil War, both sides supplied their troops with alcohol. Once the war ended, the temperance movement picked up its media strategy where it had left off, commissioning a mix of cultural works, from songs to literature, to spread their message. *Miss Belinda's Friends,* a novel published in 1885 by the New York–based National Temperance Society and Publication House, is a typical example. The novel details one community's struggles with drinking, which results in the death of a character, the loss of a family fortune, and the founding of an anti-drinking society. The author, Mary Dwinell Chellis, had developed something of a niche; her other titles included *The Temperance Doctor, Aunt Dinah's Pledge*, and *Drinking Jack and Other Stories*.

Anti-drinking songs emerged, constituting an entire genre of early American music. Songs ranged from rousing to sentimental but kept the same topic in mind. "The Drunkard's Funeral" (Wm. T. Meyer, 1876) narrates a dark morning: "As I softly hear one say, Old King Rum has one more victim they will bury here today." In G. H. Cleveland's "Hurrah for Temperance" (1877) begins, "Come now, the sun just peeps thro' the clouds / Showing to us the storm is nearly o'er / Come sign the pledge and join in our crowd, / To drive intemp'rance from our door."

The concept of "signing a temperance pledge" came into fashion in the mid-1800s, although pledges had been known for some time. In a handwritten note in a Bible, dated 1637, a Rev. R. Bolton swore that "from this day forward, to the end of my life, I will never pledge any health, nor drink a carouse, in a glass, cup, bowl or other drinking instrument whatsoever . . ."[25] The practice of making a vow to abstain from all intoxicating liquors would eventually move from temperance leagues to sober programs like Alcoholics Anonymous.

In time, the concept of making a public announcement of abstinence, even for a short time, was updated with the introduction of Dry January, Sober October, and other mass non-drinking movements.

LATE 1800S TO PROHIBITION

"Brooklyn Saloons Were Closed" read the front page of *The Journal*, a New York City tabloid. "[T]housands and thousands of residents found it impossible to obtain a drink of liquor . . . Groups of men gathered in front of many of the saloons in the afternoon discussing the new state of affairs in a dazed sort of way."

This article wasn't describing a scene from the first day of Prohibition, enacted on January. 17, 1919. The events from that Monday's front-page story took place on Sunday, March 29, 1896.

As 1896 began, the news that dominated New York, and which was covered colorfully nearly every day, had to do with what became known as the Raines Law. What the law sought to control, and how New Yorkers reacted to it, predicted not just national Prohibition but Americans' cavalier attitude toward alcohol laws.

In early January 1896, Sen. John Raines drafted a bill that would outlaw bars from opening on Sundays, and raise license fees for venues, with the goal of thinning out New York's many saloons. On March 23, 1896, the New York State Legislature passed the law, which, among other things, banned all-night licenses and restricted saloons from opening within 200 yards of schools or churches. Only hotels could serve liquor on Sundays, and they could do so only with meals. The law defined hotels as establishments with at least ten rooms.

The Raines Law was of such interest that an entire article was devoted to a detailed description of the governor's desk (mahogany, 12x7 feet, blue cloth cover) and the pen (steel, black celluloid handle, red mottling) he used to sign the bill.[26]

So began a year of enthusiastic coverage about the impacts (and open flouting) of the Raines Law. Despite the law's high profile, New Yorkers found creative ways to skirt it, which were gleefully reported by the local papers. It's hard to imagine that accounts of such exploits weren't also read by the authorities, yet the illegality went on in the open.

The Raines Law was a direct reaction to America's drinking culture, which was said to have shocked even the Europeans. In 1895, New York City's residents drank 170 million gallons of liquor, or 32 quarts per person, leading to 31,897 arrests for drunkenness. While men made up the majority (over 22,000) of those arrested, around 8,000 women were also hauled off to jail. New York's population in 1895 was 1.95 million. Given New York's 8,730 saloons and bars, that means there was one saloon for every 224 men, women, and children. Put another way, there was one saloon for every 56 adult males.

According to the *Journal*, "If concentrated, New York saloons would fill the space from Franklin & 28th Street and Seventh and First Aves." Lined up side by side, the saloons could extend from City Hall to Stamford, Connecticut, a span of 35 miles.

The Raines Law's loopholes became the focus of ingenuity. To fulfill the ten-room require-ment, saloons added ramshackle "rooms" in upper floors or expanded to neighboring spaces. (This quickly resulted in the rooms being used by unmarried couples and prostitutes; but they were also used to drink in. By December, Brooklyn alone hosted over 1,800 "sinful" hotels.) Venues began serving (and re-serving) the inedible "Raines sandwich." "In many instances one battered and veteran sandwich was served as a 'meal' at least a hundred times," the *Journal* reported. "In the East Side district such a thing as attempting to eat the 'meal' was considered sufficiently bad saloon etiquette to cause comment."[27]

Six weeks after the passing of the new law, New York spots "did not make the slightest pre-tense of observing the Raines or any other liquor law." "To get a drink, it was only necessary to sit down at a table and order it," the *Journal* said.[28] Eventually, since people weren't eating the food, some enterprising bars began serving rubber and paper versions of the "Raines sandwich."

The breezy flouting of the Raines Law stood in relief against the temperance movement, which tried, with a range of success, to cultivate a less stodgy image than the public attributed to it. The temperance movement tried to normalize the idea that one can socialize and have a good time without imbibing hard spirits. In contrast to the early colonial days, when non-alcoholic options were limited to switchels (a vinegar-based drink), coffee, teas, and other home brews, by the late 1800s the nascent cocktail age brought about more variation in non-alcoholic drink options.

Temperance cocktails were present during the late 1800s, even if they mostly took a back seat to the Manhattans, juleps, and Champagne cocktails popular during this era, which is still considered the golden age of cocktails. Jerry Thomas's seminal *Bar-Tender's Guide: How to Mix Drinks, or The Bon Vivant's Companion* (1862) featured the soda cocktail, made with soda water, sugar, and bitters. William Boothby's *Cocktail Boothby's American Bar-Tender* (1891) featured several simple no-proof drinks, among them an orgeat lemonade and soda mixed with raspberry syrup. Thomas Stuart's *Fancy Drinks and How to Mix Them* (1896) had an entire "Temperance Drinks" section, including lemonades, lemon sherbet, and soda nectar. Some years later, Harry Craddock's influential *The Savoy Cocktail Book* (1930) introduced the Keep Sober cocktail (grenadine, citron syrup, and tonic).

By the mid-1800s, non-alcoholic drinks were called "soft drinks," as opposed to their "hard" liquor siblings. According to Merriam-Webster, the first known use of "soft drink" to describe a carbonated non-alcoholic drink dates to 1843.

The forerunners of the global soft drink market began in drugstores, then moved to soda fountains. Cities like New York and Philadelphia in the 1830s were the first to try out the concept of cold fizzy waters plus sugar syrups. (In Philadelphia, the invention of fizzy lemonade is attributed to a French perfumer.)

Root beer, a drink made from the "roots" of angelica, sarsaparilla, and ginger, was advertised as a "substitute for alcoholic and malt liquors . . . superior to mineral or soda waters." Root beer "cheers but not inebriates," an 1841 advertisement read. "It may be rendered the most powerful cause in Temperance. The proprietor has fixed the price so low that it forms a much cheaper beverage than can be obtained from soda powders, or fountain or even lemon syrup and no family ought or will be without it after a trial."

In the early 1880s, entrepreneur Charles Sumner Eaton, an MIT-trained chemist, opened Thompson's Temperance Spa in Boston. The "spa," also called Temperance Bar, served phosphates, egg lemonades, and coffees. Thompson's is considered to be one of the first, and most successful, temperance saloons. According to published reports, "within five years, the saloon was selling some 1,200 egg phosphates on the most humid summer days."[29] By 1887, Thompson's was "the most crowded drinking establishment in Boston," according to a news article. (Thompson's opened several locations and stayed in business until 1958.)

Thompson's and other soda fountains struck a chord with consumers, who made these early no-proof venues as popular as taverns. "One downtown drug store centrally located sold on an average ten thousand drinks a day during the entire week," the *Journal* reported in 1896.[30] "In the shopping district as many as a thousand glasses of orange phosphate are sold a day." Celery phosphate, chocolate walnut sodas, and almond creams were among the new hot flavors that season. By 1913, over 475 million gallons, or eight billion glasses of soda water, were drunk each year. Soda sales added up to $500 million per year; there were over 100,000 soda fountains in the U.S. at the start of the twentieth century.[31]

In 1888, the *Pittsburgh Press* investigated what one could order at a "soft drink saloon." In addition to lemonades, pop, ginger ale, seltzer, and buttermilk, there was a suggestion that spiked versions of drinks could be had "with a wink." "At such places, a wink is as good as 10 cents, and one who can work his optic can get along first rate," wrote a reporter who never used the words *liquor* or *hard*, yet managed to make his point quite poetically. By the time Prohibition finally arrived, these kinds of sly practices were already hardwired into drinking culture.

Temperance taverns, a forerunner to today's alcohol-free bars, started to sprout as early as the 1830s, when existing taverns were convinced to stop selling hard spirits, according to early records from temperance societies.

A reformed tavern, stripped of its bottles, looked a bit like a coffeehouse. Coffeehouses, which date back to 1650s Europe, had been a part of American colonial life since the start, but were typically woven into taverns rather than seen standalone venues. As saloons closed, the coffeehouse stepped in as a substitute meeting place. "Coffee-Drunken New York," a 1923 feature in the *New York Times Magazine*, noted the spike in interest: "Men who drank one cup of coffee before prohibition take two now. The number of men and women who breakfast on nothing but coffee is increasing."[32] In a bit of historical haziness, coffee makers tried to unlink coffee from its tavern days: A 1916 full-page coffee ad (perhaps intentionally) misstated the famed meeting place of General George Washington as "Fraunces Coffee House," rather than Fraunces Tavern.

As World War I loomed, temperance got a major makeover around the world: It became patriotic not to drink. Sort of.

In 1914, British authorities found themselves disgusted with drunkenness among troops and civilians alike. London pubs were made to close at 10 p.m., without much impact on reports of drunkenness. In March 1915, Minister of Munitions (and future prime minister) David Lloyd George famously said, "We are fighting Germany, Austria and drink and so far as I can see the greatest of these three deadly foes is drink. It is the general feeling that if we are to settle German militarism we must first of all settle with drink." A month later, King George V banned alcohol from the royal households.

Lloyd George floated the specter of national prohibition in the United Kingdom. It was not passed, although some new laws, such as the banning of "treating" (buying other people drinks), were introduced. Russia, France, and Germany, however, banned certain spirits among troops around this time. So it's no surprise that in May 1917, one month after America joined the war, the U.S. Army announced that it was "bone dry."

This was the first, and only, war in which American troops were asked to stay sober. As of May 1917, it was a "crime to sell or give an intoxicating drink to an officer or enlisted man." Saloons and bars took no chances.

"For the first time in memory, sailors could not buy or beg a drink, and they had a gloomy evening," the *New York Times* reported. "In squads they marched up Sands Street, through Fulton, and then up Washington Street trying in every saloon and cafe to get a drink, wishing one, the more because they had been told they couldn't get it. But so far as could be ascertained, none was successful."

It's worth noting that originally, President Wilson intended the law as a wartime prohibition, so that the U.S. could conserve grain. These first steps, along with various states' dry laws, paved the way for the Volstead Act, which became the 18th Amendment, banning the manufacture, sale, and transportation of alcoholic beverages. The amendment, passed on January 16, 1919, was enacted over Wilson's veto.

In the fall of 1919, with Prohibition going into effect at the start of 1920, the Salvation Army opened a dry saloon in an old hotel in Boston, while the Episcopal Church announced a plan to open "substitute saloons" across the country. "A nice, fat bartender will preside over the soft drinks," the *New York Tribune* reported. "The brass rail will stand." Men could smoke, curse, and play cards, while "clergymen, women and sightseers" were banned.

In a nod to what by then was already ingrained American culture, church officials tacitly acknowledged the legacy and power of the tavern: "Our experience in the past has shown us that no uniform and no 'Good Hope Mission' sign will take the place of the barroom and the aproned bartender."[33]

THE MOCKTAIL ERA

Miss Judy King, an Atlanta socialite, held a trendsetting event at the Druid Hills Golf Club on a bright September day in 1942. The fashionable gathering, in honor of her sorority rushes, was a new kind of fete. It was "an innovation, in the form of a mocktail party," the *Atlanta Constitution* reported in its society pages. "The mocktail party is so called because the beverages to be served will resemble cocktails, but they will not be intoxicants."

Whether she knew it or not, Miss King was far ahead of her time.

Following the repeal of Prohibition in 1933, America was gleefully awash in liquor and cocktails, this time legally. The December 5, 1933, front page of the *New York Daily News* showed whiskey barrels stacked in a Brooklyn warehouse, as the tri-state area waited anxiously for the announcement that the 18th Amendment would, at long last, be repealed. At precisely 5:32 · p.m. Eastern time, Utah was the 36th state to ratify the 21st Amendment, overturning national Prohibition after 14 years. In New York alone, nearly seven million quarts of liquor and wine were ready in local warehouses. But with only 500 approved trucks and only 1,000 legally licensed venues, New Yorkers turned to bootleggers for one last epic party.

The December 6, 1933, *Daily News* captured the nation's mood. "You Can Drink! Repeal Voted!" read the double-height block headline. Photos of cheerful New Yorkers and a crowded wine store sat next to a shot of a smiling President Franklin Roosevelt. A two-page photo spread inside detailed New York's reaction as "the dry dam breaks" and a "swirling flood of legal liquor inundates city to quench thirst 13-years a-growing."

Given the resounding failure of Prohibition, and the ensuing giddiness following the return of legalized drinking, the conversation around non-alcoholic drinks retreated from the spotlight

for some time. The era's most talented American bartenders had long ago decamped to Europe, and it would be years, if not decades, before Americans took cocktail-making seriously again.

The drys were still a powerful lobby post-Prohibition, although they began to see the waning of their political pull. In 1936, they shifted their focus to the perils of drinking and driving, pointing out that auto accidents could hurt more people than accidents involving horse-drawn buggies. Local business groups also took up the conversation on moderation, discussing "the effects of alcohol on industrial efficiency."[34]

In the meantime, during the post-Prohibition era, "temperance" and "temperance cocktails" were no longer in vogue as phrases, although the idea of the non-alcoholic drink evolved.

Enter the mocktail.

Merriam-Webster dates the first recorded use of the term *mocktail* to 1916. According to ProQuest, a collection of 112 databases that includes over 20 million pages in over 26,000 publications dating back three centuries, *mocktail* emerged in newspapers in the 1940s. In the fall of 1941, a year before Miss King's party, a whiskey brand used *mocktail* to describe an inferior drink. "Mocktail or Cocktail?" an ad for Three Feathers blended whiskey said. In contrast to a cocktail made with Three Feathers, a mocktail had a "melted whiskey flavor that does a Now-You-Taste-It-Now-You-Don't Act . . . does disappointing things to any Manhattan." Ads for Three Feathers ran in New Jersey's *Asbury Park Evening Press* that autumn.

A curious thing happened to the non-alcoholic drink in the Prohibition era. It gained currency among fashionable ladies and became ingrained into the ethos of hospitality, both at home and in venues. Over time, knowing how to make a good non-alcoholic drink became a mark of good manners, for hostesses and bartenders alike.

As previously noted, temperance leagues were canny about getting their message out. Around the turn of the century, the leagues developed dry cocktail recipes, which were given to newspapers and women's magazines. There was, at first, resistance. In June 1895, *Good Housekeeping* warned that "there are multitudes of non-alcoholic beverages that are to be regarded with suspicion." The article went on to warn about the dangers of "filthy ice" and "doctored drinks" at soda fountains. (Only tea, lemonade, and coffee were recommended to the modern hostess.) A temperance cocktail recipe, suggested as a lively concoction for December 1916's New Year's parties, was whipped up for a New York official to taste. His verdict: "Mix carefully and pour down the sink."

But with each new generation, the tenor of the non-alcoholic drink evolved.

By 1931, knowing how to serve a temperance cocktail was key for every hostess "who is averse to the use of alcoholic preparations but is anxious to do the smart thing." "Served with all the traditional ceremony of the cocktail hour, the tomato cocktail is a delicious appetizer that relaxes your guests and sends them into dinner in a genial mood," *Chatelaine* magazine wrote in that year's June issue. The accompanying recipe, called simply Temperance Cocktail, was made by infusing tomato juice with onion, celery, parsley, lemon, and Worcestershire sauce. Modern eyes will recognize the makings of a Bloody Mary, which, according to cocktail lore, was invented three years later, in 1934, at King Cole Bar in New York's St. Regis hotel.

Following Miss King's example, by the 1950s, notices about "mocktail parties" became common among the society set, usually in the context of fundraising galas, sorority events, and charity soirees.

Fast-forward a few years, and it wasn't just fashionable women espousing moderation. "Despite all the talk about three-martini lunches, there's much less alcohol consumed over business meetings than the Internal Revenue Service might think," the *Chicago Tribune* reported in 1978. According to the National Restaurant Association, in 1978, Americans ordered alcoholic drinks on less than 10 percent of all occasions.

Ambitious executives still had to network socially, whether at business lunches or company functions. Whether as a result of the temperance movement or not, some business leaders started to realize that drinking all the time wasn't good for industry.

Many non-drinkers came up with ruses, which, ironically, were first deployed at Raines Law–era bars. Customers ordered privately from the bartender "so that no one else hears," then gave him a "knowing wink" when it was time for refills, for example. During an annual sales conference in the late 1970s, a successful businessman, described as "the president of one large Chicago-based corporation," tipped a bartender $50 to "pour all his drinks from a Smirnoff bottle filled with water."[35] An anonymous bartender told the *Chicago Tribune* that he worked many functions, including weddings and bar mitzvahs, where "almost everyone thinks everyone else is drinking . . . but almost nobody is."

In the 1980s, the no-proof drink entered wider consciousness. The *Washington Post* drafted a cheeky list of things that would be cool for 1985. In: Billy Idol, Eddie Murphy, iridescence, and portable CDs. Out: Billy Joel, Dudley Moore, glitter, and portable TVs. In: Mocktail parties. Out: Happy hours.

Mocktails began appearing in articles, as newspapers reported on universities staging parties centered around non-drinking options. Regional papers also began to cover a new kind of drink competition, where the goal was to invent new non-alcoholic sips. At first glance, these were two separate phenomena. But upon closer inspection, both the university parties and the mocktail competitions had the same agenda: to lower the prevalence of drunk driving.

The rise in drunk driving deaths in the 1980s was part of a domino effect that started in 1933. Following the repeal of Prohibition, most states linked the minimum legal drinking age to the voting age, raising it from 18 to 21. In 1942, during World War II, Congress lowered the age that young men could be drafted to 18. Nearly thirty years later, as Americans were drafted to fight in the Vietnam War, many young people protested that they were old enough to die in combat yet had no say in elections.

The 26th Amendment, passed in 1971, lowered the voting age for Americans to 18. Once 18-year-olds could vote and die for their country, however, they pressured states to also lower the drinking age. Between 1970 and 1975, nearly 30 states lowered their minimum drinking age to 18 or 19. Within a few years, however, drunk driving killed thousands of teenagers, many of whom would drink legally in one state, then drive drunk to their home state.

The temperance movement, in its waning days of power, predicted that not enough was being done to educate the public about the dangers of drinking and driving, especially around social functions like football games, house parties, and bar visits. Sadly, in the 1970s and 1980s, these fears came true. In 1981, there were more than 49,000 traffic deaths in the U.S., with about half of the accidents involving drinking, the *New York Times* reported. That's more than the 47,752 reported combat deaths during the 16-year Vietnam War.

By the early 1980s, several studies linked young drinkers with alcohol-related car accidents, while national papers put the spotlight on several high-profile tragedies. "Drunk driving is our nation's hidden epidemic," an academic at the University of Michigan's Transportation Research Institute told the *New York Times* in 1982.

Lawmakers began to feel pressure from activist groups such as Mothers Against Drunk Driving (MADD. founded in 1980). In 1984, President Reagan signed the National Minimum Drinking Age Act, which required states to raise the drinking age to 21 or risk losing some of their federal highway funding. States such as Massachusetts banned practices such as unlimited happy hours, where customers could drink all they wanted to for as little as $5.

In December 1984, the White House hosted a "mocktail party," offering an array of no-proof drinks as well as "imitation beers and wines," aiming to showcase the wide range of non-alcoholic options "in hopes of curbing drunken driving."[36] Given this context, it makes sense that the *Washington Post* dubbed "mocktail parties" as "in" for 1985, that the *Philadelphia Inquirer* covered an "Open Mocktail" fraternity party at West Chester University in April 1985, and that the University of Maryland opened the Dry Dock, an alcohol-free space for its students, in February 1986.

As for those mocktail competitions, they were often sponsored by organizations such as the American Automobile Association. AAA's Great Pretenders Mocktail Mix-Off debuted in the early 1980s and was held every December in multiple states. Regional papers covered the winning recipes and offered tips on how to spice up non-alcoholic options during the party season. AAA also published a free "party guide" that was available nationally. In a similar vein, Students Against Drunk Driving hosted mocktail parties in the 1980s, geared around prom season, while various chambers of commerce and local business groups held seminars, paid for with federal funds, that advised corporations on how to throw responsible holiday parties.

Winners of AAA's mocktail competition reflected the tastes of the bar industry in the 1980s, which had lost touch with the elegance of the pre-Prohibition drinks world. As a result, many of these Reagan-era mocktails were either simple juice-and-tonics or wildly decadent milk-shakes. In 1987, the Fuzzy Angel swept AAA's Oklahoma regionals; the recipe combined 1 scoop raspberry sherbet, 2 scoops vanilla ice cream, 3 ounces sliced peaches, 1 ounce half-and-half, 1 ounce orange juice, 1 teaspoon grated orange peel . . . and 1 tablespoon sugar. The drink was *then* garnished with whipped cream and a dusting of cinnamon. Two years later, Michigan's winning drink was the Nutcracker Marzipan Palace, a heady mix of 2 scoops Häagen-Dazs Macadamia Brittle ice cream, 2 tablespoons almond paste, 1/4 cup condensed milk, and, for some reason, 1/2 cup ginger ale. The drink was blended, topped with whipped cream and sprinkles . . . and served one.

Despite their intense offerings, the early mocktail competitions not only promoted the agenda that people shouldn't drink and drive, but they made hospitality professionals aware that there was a market of people who go out yet choose not to partake.

That growing awareness spawned a conversation around how to make the non-drinker feel included. "Presentation and equality of service are important," Barbara Heinzmann, a registered nurse, wrote in a 1985 New Year's Eve op-ed in the *Orlando Sentinel*.[37] "I have had stemware whisked away by the host when it was learned I wasn't having wine or a mixed drink and replaced by a not so elegant tumbler. I'm not out to chip anyone's crystal with ice cubes, but I do appreciate being treated like the rest of the guests."

"I have learned two important things: First, I can and do have a good time without alcohol," Ms. Heinzmann added. "Second, if a nonalcoholic choice is available and given equal status when offered, many people will take advantage of it."

Like Miss King before her, Ms. Heinzmann predicted the next big concept in no-proof drinking: the radical idea that non-drinkers should be treated with respect.

DRY JANUARY AND THE RISE OF THE NEW MODERATION

Ever try to have a non-alcoholic drink at a party and have your friends ask if you don't want to change your mind? That's not new, because for centuries we've been hardwired to link socializing with drinking.

"It was really hard," Lala Alvarez told the *Los Angeles Times* in December 2005.[38] "I told people I was laying off the alcohol, and there was this pressure—"'Have a drink with us! This drink tastes fantastic!' I'm like, stop it." Alvarez was part of a small gym group that tried out a novel experiment; that fall, members took a month off drinking. Their personal trainer called it Sober October. The disciplined athletes had no issues not drinking, but it was the peer pressure they found hardest to navigate.

Another Sober October athlete told the *L.A. Times*, "I figured everyone around me is a mature adult. But it's a bonding thing, that's how they look at it." The article described how she had to "hold a glass of wine in her hand to make [friends] feel comfortable."

Trying to skip out on drinking while at a bar often feels strange. Not to the abstainer, but to everyone else around that person. That's not an accident, given our history.

As a result of an occasionally well-founded bias against water, the high expense and low availability of non-alcoholic options like tea and coffee, and an etiquette born out of centering civic life in taverns, colonial Americans wove drinking into the fabric of socializing from the earliest days of this nation. While some people will scoff that practices dating to the 1700s

can't possibly have impact on our modern age, stepping into many social situations today means walking into long-accepted conventions about how one acts.

In post-Revolutionary America, "drinking became a symbol of egalitarianism," historian W. J. Rorabaugh wrote.[39] "All men were equal before the bottle, and no man was allowed to refuse to drink." Refusing to drink in social settings was a serious social offense, and it suggested that "the abstainer thought himself to be better than other people." Offending one's community carried serious repercussions; Rorabaugh noted that "a gang of lusty Kentuckians angry with an abstinent comrade is reputed to have roasted him to death."

The temperance movement, which began with religious leaders, didn't help moderation's boring image. The drys were historically seen as killjoy scolds, and there's certainly some truth to that. While there were places, such as coffeehouses, where people socialized without drinking liquor, for the most part even sophisticated contemporary drinkers tended to arch an eyebrow toward anything that hinted of a holier-than-thou abstainer.

Given that English drinking culture heavily influenced early American patterns, it makes sense that modern British and American drinking cultures were often in lockstep. So when a new temperance trend started gaining steam in the U.K., the skepticism about non-drinkers felt familiar.

"DRY JANUARY FUTILE," British tabloid *The Sun* blared in one of the first headlines of 2012. "Laying off the booze for January is a 'medically futile' gesture, health experts warned yesterday." The full context of the medical opinion, in light of skyrocketing alcoholic liver disease rates in the U.K., was that people should take a more mindful account of their drinking year-round, rather than just focusing small efforts during one month. That nuance was lost if one just scanned the headline, however.

The concept of Dry January, a monthlong drinks abstinence after holiday season indulgence, began colloquially in Britain in the 2000s, where it was part of the post-holiday quiet period. Between 2000 and 2012, the vast majority of "dry January" mentions in global newspapers appeared in weather-related articles, according to Factiva. One of the first non-drinking mentions of the phrase appeared in 2005. In 2011, of the 163 articles in Factiva's database that cite "dry January," just six mentions were related to drinking.

That changed in the fall of 2012, when nonprofit Alcohol Change UK (then called Alcohol Concern) announced their splashy new campaign.[40] The first official Dry January debuted in 2013 and raised money for charity by having people take a non-drinking pledge that was financially supported by friends and relatives. Fueled in part by high drinking rates, the charity sought to raise awareness about the 4.5 million days that Britons went to work hungover each year.

The concept of making a public vow to abstain from drinking, of course, was an updated take on the temperance pledge, which dates back to at least 1637.[41] A popular practice during the 1800s temperance wave, a pledge was a way to hold oneself accountable to the promise of quitting alcohol.

In the early Dry January articles, the conversation around taking a vacation from drinking, and how one socializes while abstaining, was played out in the press. *Telegraph* columnist Peter Oborne found "the prospect of doing Dry January simply terrifying. In particular, I am dreading going to parties." Columnist Bryony Gordon was dubbed "Boring Bryony" by her own colleagues when she chose to try out the experiment. "The truth is, I have quite enjoyed not drinking," she later wrote. Many articles followed this pattern: Someone who takes time off from drinking comes to enjoy it, but they always encounter peer pressure.

Dry January is a callback to the temperance pledge, so it's not surprising that it managed to stir up longstanding resentments against dry drinkers.

As 2015 kicked off, *The Independent* columnist Lucy Hunter Johnston railed against the "smug chorus" of January non-drinkers asking for lime-and-sodas, writing: "To which the only suitable response is a withering look and a swift brace of shots." Echoing a sentiment like those found in Rorabaugh's history book, Johnston opined that not drinking means "you will become such a dreadful bore that no one will want to spend any time with you."

"Are we really so infantile and unable to manage our own health that we have to be peer pressured into quitting for a month to raise money for charity?" Ms. Johnston wrote. "The short-term sober even have a name for themselves: Dry Athletes, a label so twee it makes me want to puke."

Despite the early critics, Dry January took off like a rocket. According to Alcohol Change, what started with 4,000 signatures in 2013 swelled to an estimated five million Britons in 2020. Americans took to the trend enthusiastically: An estimated one in five Americans practiced Dry January in 2019. It's a phenomenon fueled by the social media age; between 2015 and 2019, Dry January mentions in social media went up by 1,083 percent, according to market research firm Mintel.[42]

As for critics pointing out that one month of abstinence won't have much health impact, those who took time off in January report drinking less throughout the year, according to research published by the University of Sussex in 2018. [43] The study found that 82 percent of respondents reconsidered their drinking habits, while 71 percent concluded "they don't need a drink to enjoy themselves." Drinking days fell from 4.3 to 3.3 per week, and the frequency of being drunk dropped from 3.4 days per month to 2.1 per month.

In 2018, *The Lancet* published an analysis of alcohol use data in 195 countries between 1990 and 2016.[44] The conclusion, which was picked up in papers around the world: No amount of alcohol is safe. Just one drink a day can raise your risk for health issues.[45] A rival study from the National Institutes of Health sought to prove that one cocktail or beer per day could protect against disease, but the study was shut down in June 2018 after the *New York Times* reported that the lead researcher was working closely with the alcohol industry and secured more than $100 million from beer and liquor brands to fund the trial.[46,47]

By the start of 2020, as more consumers began to take the wellness trend seriously, the tenor of its coverage in the press had mostly changed. *USA Today* wrote: "A 'Dry January' is good for more than just a healthy liver." From the *Washington Times*: "Booze is out and 'sober curiosity' is in as people around the world participate in Dry January and voluntarily abstain from alcohol for the month." *Cosmopolitan* wrote: "Listen, fad diets and detoxes are lame. But the Dry January tradition, which got its start in the UK in 2012, is actually pretty legit." And from *Financial News*: "A series of booze-fueled controversies in the City in 2019 make Dry January even more pertinent this year."

There was also a fresh round of research looking at the impact of alcohol. In January 2020, researchers found that the rate of alcohol-related deaths per year doubled between 1999 and 2017; nearly one million deaths in that timespan were categorized as alcohol-related.[48]

Dry January is not the only time people put liquor on hold. In addition to Sober October, other events occasionally pop up in the press, such as Dry July and No-Booze November. In general, drinkers of all stripes are now reassessing how and when they drink. "Every year I do a Dry January but I don't last the whole month," David Purcell, bar director at NoMad Los Angeles, says "The result is that now I take the first week of every month off."

What first started with Dry January and Sober October has given people an opportunity to negotiate drinking (mostly) without judgment. As the *New York Times*'s Alex Williams described it in a June 2019 feature story: "Many will tell you they never had a drinking problem. They just had a problem with drinking."[49]

The swelling ranks of mindful moderates points to a shift in culture, and is leading to business opportunities for a new kind of savvy entrepreneur.

Listen Bar came about when founder Lorelei Bandrovschi tried to complete a Dry January and was dismayed at the lack of choices for non-drinkers. Ben Branson founded Seedlip because he wanted sophisticated non-alcoholic options while dining out. Scottish beer brand BrewDog opened a booze-free bar in London in January 2020. A new spate of non-alcoholic drink brands with sophisticated flavor palates, such as Kin Euphorics, Casamara Club, Ceder's, Everleaf, and Ritual Zero Proof, appeal to the mindful drinker, who may still sometimes drink. Even corporate giants such as Anheuser-Busch are stepping in to serve this new market; in 2020, Anheuser-Busch released Golden Road's Non-Alcoholic Mango Cart beer.

The noise around Dry January might be getting too loud for some industries.

French winemakers, who sell over 3.7 billion bottles of wine each year, were scandalized in the fall of 2019 when the French health minister suggested France might replicate Britain's Dry January concept in 2020. President Emmanuel Macron "let it be known" that the dry month would not be happening among the French. French superchef Alain Ducasse publicly stepped into the fray that January, slashing prices for top vintages in several of his restaurants to get people to drink wine "by the bottle rather than by the glass." The chef was said to be "appalled to see customers in New York order iced tea with their lunch instead of wine."[50]

Emboldened by the French, British brewers called on Prime Minister Boris Johnson to end the health initiative, citing "struggling breweries and pubs."[51]

THE AGE OF THE ZERO-PROOF COCKTAIL

At the 2020 Academy Awards, as Bong Joon Ho's *Parasite* made history as the first non-English film to win Best Picture and Best Director, Hollywood's A-list sipped on Piper-Heidsieck Champagne, of course. They were also served a class act no-proof martini made by star bartender Charles Joly. The zero-proof drink featured Seedlip, basil giardiniera oil, and "filthy brine." Served up in a coupe, it is an elegant drink that's visually indistinguishable from its gin cohorts in every way.

Joly has served non-alcoholic drinks for the past few years at the Oscars and the Emmys, where he is the official bartender. Nearly all the guests at these awards ceremonies try the no-proof options, he says. He takes extreme care, from designing flavor profiles to choosing glassware and garnishes, to ensure that his non-alcoholic drinks are on the same plane as their boozy counterparts. "Why can't we have intelligent adult choices that don't have alcohol in them?" Joly asks.

"This is a black-tie affair," he adds. "We're adults. What am I going to do, give a Shirley Temple to a thirty-five-year-old person?"

Joly's Oscars drinks, in style and presentation, are representative of how far the non-alcoholic drink has evolved from its early mocktail days. Around 2015, when the craft cocktail revolution finally turned its attention to the sophisticated non-alcoholic drink, one of the first things to go was the old name, along with the old ways of thinking.

Mocktails, as a name, is out. In general, bartenders take issue with the term because "mock" is defined as a mimicry or lesser version of what it replicates. There's also "to mock," as in "to shame or make fun of."

At Bibo Ergo Sum in Los Angeles, owner Tait Forman says that a phrase that implies inferior quality undermines hospitality. "If we're saying we care about cocktails, but these over here are 'inferior cocktails,' that doesn't live up to our ethos of serving good products," Forman says. "You are putting out a good product, with as much care as the next product, which may or may not have alcohol."

"I hate that word," Dave Arnold says of *mocktail.* Arnold, one of the most highly respected names in bartending and a co-owner of Existing Conditions in New York, says he became interested in tackling non-alcoholic drinks after hearing a bartender dismiss a drink he was making as "just a mocktail." "I was like, 'Wow, that really sucks. I hope I never treat my guests with that level of disrespect.'"

Arnold is far from alone. Declan McGurk, the head of the award-winning American Bar at The Savoy Hotel, recalls going out around 2013 with his then-pregnant wife. "We went into a bar and the bartender really didn't have an appetite for it," he says. "It was always in the back of my mind, 'How can you still offer that experience to a guest just because they are not drinking alcohol?' When Seedlip first came onto the market, we jumped on it straight away."

"When we launched [in 2015], there were no other non-alcoholic spirits," Seedlip founder Ben Branson says. "In the U.K., there were one or two non-alcoholic beers. You definitely couldn't find a non-alcoholic cocktail on a menu. And you would definitely be laughed at if you asked for a non-alcoholic cocktail."

Seedlip is credited with kick-starting a widespread reconsideration of the no-proof drink and forcing hospitality experts to become aware of some of their biases. "When Seedlip came out, I remember comments from bartenders being like, 'What the fuck is this,'" says Giuseppe González, a bartender who has been open about his longtime sobriety. "And I thought, 'Why do you care? They came up with something. Why are you upset about it?'

"People get defensive about not drinking," he adds. "There's legitimate anger behind it and I don't know why."

For those bartenders that do explore the zero-proof drink, what makes today's non-alcoholic drink different from the mocktails of the past comes down to respect, for the drink as well as for the consumer. If a Manhattan is made with premium ingredients and served in a vintage glass, then so can a non-alcoholic drink.

Alex Kratena was head bartender at London's Artesian Bar when it landed as number one on the World's 50 Best Bars list and stayed there for four consecutive years. In 2013, Kratena and his team integrated their non-alcoholic drinks alongside Artesian's traditional boozy drinks in the menu, rather than list them in a separate section. "For me, it was about making a huge statement," says Kratena, who now co-owns Tayēr + Elementary in London. "It's not about alcohol; it's about deliciousness and flavor."

"We realized that many people actually were not able to tell [the drinks apart]," he adds. "There were people that were coming for several months and only after five months, they find out that their favorite thing was non-alcoholic."

At Manhattan's Existing Conditions, all drinks, non-alcoholic or not, are made using techniques that can't be replicated at home such as centrifugal clarification. "When [a drink] is served, there is no indication whether it's alcoholic or not," Dave Arnold says. "We made certain there is no telltale way of serving the non-alcoholic drink, so you can't tell them apart."

As the no-proof drink evolves, so do the occasions and spaces for them. An alcohol-free bar may once have seemed like a punchline, but it's now one of the most talked-about developments in hospitality. It's emerged in response to everything that's come before it.

Temperance taverns date back to the late 1800s, but they never gained widespread appeal or lost their church-sanctioned goody-goody imprimatur. Turn-of-the-century soda fountains and coffeehouses became popular meeting places, but they weren't necessarily geared toward nightlife and they didn't have the sex appeal of lounging in a dark bar with attractive bartenders shaking up crisp drinks.

But there were early signs, in the 2010s, that change was afoot. In 2013, two New Yorkers came up with the idea of hosting a dawn dance party with no alcohol. "No one knew what it was, and we also didn't know exactly what it would become," Daybreaker cofounder Matthew Brimer told *Newsday* in 2016. "It was the most wonderful, healthy, energetic, most positive party we'd ever been to. It worked." Daybreaker started with one predawn party in New York in 2013; it's now expanded into sunrise and sunset parties in cities all over the world, including Tokyo, Buenos Aires, Mexico City, and Sydney. One thing is consistent across all the events: "We don't need alcohol," per the brand's website.

Daybreaker's parties don't feature cocktails, but their popularity points to the beginning of a market that's increasingly comfortable with socializing without liquor.

"The whole controlled drinking movement is very much a modern phenomenon," Fever-Tree CEO Charles Gibb says. Before helming the drinks mixer, Gibb was CEO of Belvedere Vodka, where he was front and center in nightlife culture. "In the '80s, '90s, early 2000s, extreme hedonism was right at the core. In the vodka world, it was all about showing off, the big-party, high-energy consumerism."

"In the last five years, we're seeing a move toward controlled drinking," he adds. "We still want to drink but I might take five days off, a month off, six weeks. I still want to go out but I don't want to be stuck at home. I still want to be in the bar environment."

Enter Listen Bar. What started as a five-day pop-up in the fall of 2018 turned into a monthly residency in the basement of a Lower East Side bar in 2019.

It's not surprising that, at launch and even now, the bar has its skeptics. "You don't say, 'Cheers,' with a glass of juice," a bar manager sneered to the *Wall Street Journal* about the no-proof concept.[52]

Plenty of Listen Bar's customers clink glasses throughout the night, since the zero-proof drinks, created by star bartenders like Dead Rabbit's Jack McGarry, are mixed in the same spirit, so to speak, as traditionally boozy drinks. Throughout 2019, Listen Bar was one of New York's most talked-about new bars, covered in the press as the vanguard for the mindful drinking movement.

At the start of 2020, riding a wave of popularity and global demand, the no-proof bar announced a world tour starting in late spring, in which bars across the United States and Europe would host Listen Bar's staff for short pop-up events. Sadly, the tour was put on hold following the global coronavirus outbreak.

LET'S MEET FOR A DRINK
How Alcohol Influences Socializing

We've all said it at some point: "Let's meet for a drink." In contrast to "Let's meet for coffee" (which is informal and suggests a short amount of time) or "Let's have dinner" (which is more formal and structured), "meeting up for a drink" encompasses the full spectrum of interactions, from old friendships to business meetings to new romances. It's open-ended, and it could lead into dinner, or multiple stops in other venues.

Seedlip founder Ben Branson points out that in the phrase "Let's meet for a drink" or "I'm not drinking tonight," the drink is assumed to mean only alcohol. An alcoholic beverage is the default definition of "a drink," in the social sense. This makes people who are trying to abstain or be moderate seem like outliers. The zero-proof drinker is, by current social conventions, the one who has to explain her choices or make concessions. (Every bartender has a story of a woman who will whisper an order for a no-proof drink, confiding to a stranger that she is pregnant, while hiding the news from friends.)

As the zero-proof movement gives people a reason to take a step back from drinking at every occasion, liquor's carefree image and its requisite requirement at parties might be up for reconsideration.

Social media is heavy with messages that frame alcohol as essential ("Drink each day that ends in y") and transformative ("All my problems could be solved by a swim-up margarita bar"; "Life is too short to drink responsibly"). In *Quit Like a Woman,* Holly Whitaker outlines the ways alcohol has seeped into women's lives, not just as an occasional celebratory tool but as an accessory to everyday life, on the same level as coffee. Liquor is a symbol of women's freedom, yet it's also the crutch for harried moms who feel they need to drink to deal with

children, it's the tonic that working women reach for after a long day, and it's the elixir that binds female friendships. Jokes about "liquid diets" are placed next to images of wineglasses as big as soup bowls.

On the other end of the spectrum, the impact of alcohol is hard to miss. Nearly the entire reality-TV genre, for example, is predicated on making entertainment out of people unraveling after heavy drinking. Dating shows like *The Bachelor* franchises stage what amounts to hours-long open bars and then record the results. Contestants will be edited to seem incoherent, to comedic effect, but it's not always clear how much alcohol they consume. One season of *Bachelor in Paradise* was briefly shut down following allegations of sexual misconduct; producers came under fire for letting two contestants drink to excess and then taping the resulting hookup.

Bravo TV, which produces the *Real Housewives* franchises, has turned alcohol overconsumption into ratings success, albeit from filming the destructive nature of drunk decisions. Palm Beach police took New York Real Housewife Luann de Lesseps into custody for disorderly intoxication and resisting arrest in late 2017; the fallout over that arrest (and an embarrassing dash-cam video) formed the arc of the following seasons of her show.

On the 2020 season of Bravo's *Below Deck*, cast members were taped getting so drunk they had to be physically carried back to their ship on more than one occasion. That same season, an incoherently drunk male cast member lunged for his female colleague, and when held back was so enraged that he punched a van door several times. *Vanderpump Rules* features a group of Los Angeles friends who drink with abandon in nearly every episode, resulting in physical fights, drunken tirades, broken friendships, and even lost jobs. One of the show's stars, Lala Kent, is one of the few sober voices in reality TV; she said she sought help after a bender ended with her breaking a hurricane-proof window while naked.

There are suggestions that sobriety is on its way to becoming a cultural touchpoint, especially among the young. In late March 2020, twenty-one-year-old recording artist Conan Gray released "Wish You Were Sober," a glittering synth-pop anthem layered with earnest lyrics: "Don't take a hit, don't kiss my lips / And please don't drink more beer." The photogenic Texas native with cut-glass cheekbones also sings, "Kiss me in the seat of your Rover / Real sweet, but I wish you were sober." Gray, whose debut studio album was lauded by Billboard, Apple Music, and Taylor Swift, told reporters that he wrote "Wish You Were Sober" out of frustration over a crush who would only be affectionate when they drank heavily.

Given these far-from-glamorous images of the effects of drinking, it's not hard to imagine that many people, including younger generations, are choosing to slow down their drinking or cut it out altogether.

"When you're just going with the flow, you don't realize how powerful the current is," Lorelei Bandrovschi says of messages to drink all the time. "It takes taking yourself out of it to notice all of the subtle nudges in your life that make alcohol a default choice." The no-proof movement is prompting people to "perk up our antenna up and say, 'Well, do we? Do we need that everywhere all the time? Maybe not.'"

"When I started with Seedlip, a lot of people would talk about 'What's the point?' Æcorn cofounder and Seedlip ambassador Claire Warner says. "I have no problem with people drinking. But just by existing we are challenging this idea that maybe there's a problem if you meet someone and you can't drink. Why can't we give ourselves permission to not drink? And have that be okay?"

The mindful drinking movement doesn't necessarily mean cutting out alcohol all the time. But it does mean recognizing that there's something liberating about moderation, especially since drinking choices are often framed as either extreme debauchery or cold sobriety.

"It's really important that we start teaching everyone that going out to a bar doesn't mean you have to get wasted," Pamela Wiznitzer, a respected bar consultant, says. "Going out to a bar if you don't drink doesn't have to be an awkward interaction."

Mindful drinking is capturing a wider audience each day. The so-called sober-curious movement got a push by Ruby Warrington's best-selling book of the same name. Warrington founded Club Soda, a New York–based wellness organization that stages non-alcoholic events. In the U.K., the Mindful Drinking Festival has held panel discussions, classes, and tastings in London since 2017. Holly Whitaker founded Tempest, an online sobriety school and wellness program, based on what she found was lacking when she decided to go sober.

While Whitaker's Tempest is designed with full sobriety in mind, many of its key messages apply to even the moderate, or occasional, drinker. "Most of us just assume that we are supposed to make alcohol work in our lives," Whitaker told *Vogue* in May 2019. "I think a lot of people are starting to understand that it doesn't have to."

With several Dry Januarys under her belt, Listen Bar's Bandrovschi says she's gained a new perspective on drinking. "It's not about taking away alcohol," she says. "It's about creating room in your social life to include not drinking. Once you create room for that, you start wanting to give that little corner more and more space."

WHAT'S NEXT
The Evolution of Zero-Proof Drinking

It's taken hundreds of years, but it's finally okay to order a non-alcoholic drink at a bar. The change is coming from bartenders, who now equate crafting thoughtful no-proof options with proper hospitality, but it's mostly spurred by consumers themselves, who expect bars to provide a range of drink options, no questions asked.

While you can't talk about today's no-proof movement without referencing the early temperance movements, what's different now is where the momentum is coming from. Whereas temperance-era churches and social organizations sought to mandate how entire communities should or should not drink, the impetus behind the neo-moderation movement is coming from individuals themselves. This time, there's no sanctimonious group policing personal choices. Alcohol Change UK, which runs Dry January, puts out facts about the effects of alcohol consumption and offers guidance on how to cut back on drinking, but it doesn't lecture people into quitting.

Framing moderation or abstinence as an individual choice, rather than an imposition of rules, can be powerful and even liberating. Take, for example, the Straight Edge movement. In 1981, a song by Minor Threat kicked off a movement within punk rock culture. The 45-second song, "Straight Edge," espouses a clear anti-drug sentiment; stridently vowing to "never use a crutch," the song became the rallying cry for an entire subculture of kids who didn't drink or smoke. In a world that marketed liquor and cigarettes as essential and glamorous, not using any kind of intoxicants was the ultimate rebellion against mainstream society.

Some Straight Edgers also avoided caffeine and prescription medicine, while others practiced veganism and vegetarianism. A separate group, Vegan Straight Edge, emerged in the 1990s.

(Veganism as a lifestyle dates back to the 1940s.) Counterculture cafés blossomed in the 1980s and 1990s to cater to these emerging trends in food and drink.

Because it's anti-capitalist and insular, Straight Edge (or "sXe") didn't gain widespread traction outside of its subculture. As it evolved, some sXe factions also got more extreme, stifling the trend from going outside of its small groups. Still, at its core, the Straight Edge movement's choice to not drink or take drugs was a rejection of consumerist culture, and it's that particular tenet that feels familiar to the contemporary zero-proof drinker, who might feel exhausted by the limitless messages to drink all the time.

Additionally, the idea that alternative diets can influence the food industry at large can be seen in the mainstreaming of vegetarian and vegan lifestyles. As with Dry January, "Veganuary" is a growing trend that asks consumers to try going vegan at the start of the year. In 2019, over a quarter million Americans took a pledge to eat vegan in January; taking a month to be vegan is similar to practicing Meatless Mondays, a food trend that emerged to call attention to the environmental and health impacts of the meat industry.

The food industry's eventual embrace of veganism is important to the zero-proof movement, because veganism (and more recently, the gluten-free diet) was also met with skepticism when consumers began seeking out vegan foods in restaurants. Today, every restaurant understands that their menus need to include vegetarian, vegan, and gluten-free options.

"Diets once considered alternative are now the norm, so expect to see gluten-free, dairy-free, vegetarian, vegan, and keto options become menu mainstays," the 2020 Kimpton Hotels & Restaurants annual culinary and cocktail survey concludes. "According to 31 percent of chefs surveyed, it's no longer enough to have just one or two of these options on the menu."

The vegan and gluten-free menu is the food analogy to the no-proof movement; these choices may never overtake the mainstream, but more consumers are coming to expect a range of culinary options wherever they go, no matter if it's the local coffee shop or a fine dining establishment.

"It's not the guest's fault if they want to have something that isn't what you want them to have," Seedlip founder Ben Branson says. "If I don't want to drink alcohol, are you telling me there's something wrong with me?" Branson's question isn't always rhetorical: While I was researching this book, my best friend was expecting her first baby. While she was out at a trendy Manhattan restaurant, the waiter reacted to her request for a non-alcoholic drink by saying, "What's wrong? Don't you like alcohol?" She curtly explained that she was pregnant.

As with vegan dishes, offering a range of no-proof options on a menu is good hospitality, but it's also smart business. In 2019, Distill Ventures, a drinks accelerator and early investor in Seedlip, published a paper on the non-alcoholic space. Among the findings: Searches for "non-alcoholic" spiked 81 percent between 2018 and 2019, according to Google Trends, while searches for "mocktail" went up 42 percent in the same time period.

"A lot of this is consumer led," Distill Ventures portfolio director Heidi Otto says. "As you see what people are searching for, it feels like people aren't drinking much alcohol, but we find the data to be different. It's not so much that people are stopping alcohol, it's that they want a choice." She notes that nearly 60 percent of U.K. consumers switch back and forth between alcoholic and non-alcoholic drinks when they go out, as opposed to 29 percent who only order spirits. "It's about drinking better," she adds. "A more sophisticated, more elevated experience."

Hotels, which often have bars that are open all day as well as international clientele, were the first to showcase sophisticated no-proof drinks. "Having a cocktail menu that's purely about alcohol-focused cocktails is really going to be missing something," notes Declan McGurk of American Bar in London's Savoy hotel. "Years ago no one would have said, 'Oh, I'm not going to drink tonight,'" he adds. "Everyone would be drinking, that was just the way it was. [But today,] you shouldn't have to go into a bar and feel like you have to drink alcohol."

The emerging drinks category will be the new standard for innovation for bartenders. If the early wave of mocktails were heavy-handed candy confections and the current drinks are non-alcoholic riffs on existing standards, the future of no-proof could take off in boundary-pushing new directions.

"It's important for bartenders to move beyond the classic drinks," Alex Kratena says. Rather than trying to copy classic templates, such as daiquiris, Kratena suggests looking at how creative takes on hydrosols, or floral waters, can be used to create new flavor profiles that aren't pale mimics of boozy standards.

Just as the vegetarian and vegan world has sparked product innovation, including nut milks and plant-based meat substitutes, the next generation of zero-proof drinks will likely move from merely copying existing drink options to discovering new concoctions that reference a range of sources.

"So often [no-proof drinks are] seen as the absence of something instead of the presence of something," Maison Premiere beverage director William Elliott says. "People will add things that vaguely remind them of alcohol. If I were not to drink alcohol, I don't think I would want things that remind me of alcohol. I'd want to find new things that color my palate differently."

"To use the food analogy, people once based dishes around protein," says acclaimed London bartender Ryan Chetiyawardana. "For a long time, people did the same thing with drinks.

I have booze and I base everything around that, instead of asking, 'How do I create harmony in a different way?'"

"I think that shift in thinking is very valuable for the industry," he adds. "We need to have that different approach."

In the bigger picture, it's not just drinks or menus that will change in tandem with the no-proof movement, but venues themselves.

"There's a whole generation right now who are not drinking at all," Æcorn cofounder Claire Warner says. "If you play the tape forward, what are bars and restaurants going to do when they are catering to people who have never had an experience with alcohol? What will they serve? What will be the flavors? At the moment, we are referencing established alcohol flavors and style, but in the future they might not be relevant."

A hint of a more sensitive no-proof approach debuted in January 2020, when Minneapolis's acclaimed Marvel Bar began an "exploration series" on dry drinks. Every four months, Marvel deep-dives into one topic, with a dedicated menu. At the start of 2020, Marvel went all in on non-alcoholic drinks, including showcasing a drink made with macerated milkweed flowers that had been foraged the summer before and a dark drink that combined mushrooms with cherries. "It's called the Agatha," Marvel head bartender Peder Schweigert says. "It's not necessarily trying to replicate red wine but it's trying to give you some of the same emotions. It's interesting, it's funky. More like an old-world red than the juice-forward things that are out there."

It's what Marvel did with decor that could point to the future of the no-proof-inclusive space. Typically, the back bar at Marvel features over 400 spirits bottles, glassware, and books. But walking into a space full of bottles during Dry January can be overwhelming, so for the entirety of the dry series, Marvel's owners replaced their back bar with fresh flowers. "If you walk into a bar and you're presented with flowers and books, that's a lot more welcoming," Schweigert says.

In the future, it's entirely possible we won't even need a Dry January, not because it's "futile," as its early critics harped, but because taking time off from drinking will be second nature and completely mainstream. "The goal is normal," Seedlip's Branson says. "The goal is a balance of choice. So it's not a talking point.

"It doesn't matter what you order because you're going to get a great drink regardless."

A NOTE ABOUT RECIPES

The following recipes are the work of the bartenders credited and the bars they worked in at the time. Some people have since moved on from the bars listed on the recipe credit, as talented people tend to do. Around half of the recipes in this collection are original and were created specifically for this book, while others were on bar menus but may no longer be at the time of publication. A small handful of recipes are adaptations of earlier versions. For smaller ingredient quantities, options for grams and ounces are included, to allow for more precision in measuring.

BRIGHT & REFRESHING

GRAPEFRUIT JULEP

Joseph Hall, *Satan's Whiskers, London*

Charming and refreshing, this drink puts a spotlight on the best parts of the julep: the bracing bite of fresh mint, a snap of fresh citrus, and the fun of crushed ice. An undertone of honey guarantees you won't miss the bourbon.

Scant 2½ ounces fresh grapefruit juice
½ ounce Honey Syrup (1:1) (page 236)
2 teaspoons Simple Syrup (1:1) (page236)
2 teaspoons fresh lime juice
Scant ½ teaspoon grenadine
4 fresh mint leaves
Crushed ice (see page 16)
1 grapefruit half-moon, for garnish
1 fresh mint sprig, for garnish

In a cocktail shaker, combine the grapefruit juice, honey syrup, simple syrup, lime juice, grenadine, and mint leaves. Fill with ice, shake, then strain into a tall, chilled 12-ounce Collins glass filled with crushed ice. Garnish with the grapefruit and mint sprig and serve with a straw.

Makes 1 drink

IMPERIAL BUCK

Joseph Hall, *Satan's Whiskers, London*

There's something universally pleasant about fresh pineapple juice. Add a kick of ginger plus a touch of fizz, and you have an instant crowd pleaser.

"This drink is rich, guilt-free, and bursting with flavor," Joseph Hall says. "Plus, it makes you feel good about your life."

2 ounces fresh pineapple juice
1/2 ounce fresh lime juice
2 teaspoons Simple Syrup (1:1)
　(page 236)
2 teaspoons Ginger Syrup
　(page 238)
Chilled Fever-Tree ginger ale,
　for topping
1 fresh pineapple wedge,
　for garnish
1 fresh mint sprig, for garnish

In a cocktail shaker, combine the pineapple juice, lime juice, and syrups. Fill with ice and shake. Strain into a chilled 12-ounce highball glass filled with ice, then top with ginger ale. Garnish with the pineapple wedge and mint sprig.

Makes 1 drink

BIRD OF PARADISE

Salvatore Maggio, *The Franklin London–Starhotels Collezione, London*

A straightforward and accessible drink, Salvatore Maggio's Bird of Paradise is a great place to start your non-alcoholic cocktail journey. The bell pepper and arugula lend an herbaceousness while the unfiltered apple juice makes this a not too sweet yet approachable drink.

4 thin slices yellow bell pepper
3 arugula leaves
2 teaspoons agave nectar
5 ounces unfiltered apple juice
1/2 ounce fresh lemon juice
1 thin slice yellow bell pepper,
    for garnish
1 arugula leaf, for garnish

In a cocktail shaker, muddle 4 slices of the bell pepper and 3 arugula leaves with the agave nectar. Add the apple juice and lemon juice. Fill with ice and shake hard until the ice breaks up. Double strain (through a fine-mesh strainer, as well as the shaker's own strainer) into a tall 12-ounce Collins glass filled with ice. Garnish with the remaining bell pepper slice and arugula leaf.

Makes 1 drink

FROZEN MOTION

Devon Tarby, *Bibo Ergo Sum, Los Angeles*

The West Coast, with its fair weather and breezy lifestyle, was an early adopter of the no-proof movement. The debut menu at Los Angeles's Bibo Ergo Sum featured a version of this zippy number, which crackles with citrus and baking spices.

1¼ ounces Seedlip Spice 94 distilled non-alcoholic spirit (available at specialty stores and from Amazon)

1 ounce fresh lime juice, strained through a fine-mesh sieve to remove the pulp

1 ounce Cinnamon Syrup (page 237)

¼ teaspoon Ginger Syrup (page 238)

4 ounces chilled seltzer

1 grapefruit twist, for garnish

In a cocktail shaker, combine the Seedlip, lime juice, cinnamon syrup, and ginger syrup. Fill with ice and shake briskly. Double or fine-strain into a chilled 12-ounce flute or wineglass and gently stir in the seltzer. Squeeze the oil from the grapefruit twist over the drink, then drop it in.

Makes 1 drink

FAIRBANKS FIZZ

Daniel Sabo, *Lumière Brasserie at the Fairmont Century Plaza, Century City*

Dark & Stormy fans, this is the drink for you. Pomegranate molasses, used in Middle Eastern cuisine, is a thick, fragrant syrup with a touch of smoke; deployed in this drink, the syrup mimics rum's depths for a zero-proof cocktail you'll linger over.

1 ounce Seedlip Spice 94 distilled non-alcoholic spirit (available at specialty stores and from Amazon)
½ ounce pomegranate molasses
½ ounce fresh lime juice
4 ounces chilled Fever-Tree ginger beer
1 lime wheel, for garnish

In a cocktail shaker, combine the Seedlip, pomegranate molasses, and lime juice; add a few ice cubes and shake briefly. Add the ginger beer, swirl gently once, then strain into a chilled 12-ounce double rocks glass filled with ice. Garnish with the lime wheel and serve.

Makes 1 drink

COFFEE PUNCH

David Paz, *Xaman, Mexico City*

The coffee tonic is one of the bar world's current fascinations, in part because of the drink's versatility and day-to-night appeal. In David Paz's version, you'll find a drink with a long finish, aromas of marmalade and brown sugar, plus a satisfying astringency.

1¾ ounces high-quality cold brew coffee, chilled
Scant ¾ ounce Fig Syrup (recipe follows)
2 teaspoons fresh lime juice
Chilled Fever-Tree club soda, for topping
Pinch of ground cardamom, for garnish

In a cocktail shaker, combine the coffee, fig syrup, and lime juice. Fill with ice and shake briskly. Strain into a chilled 12-ounce Collins glass filled with ice. Pour club soda into the shaker, swirl, then top off the glass. Garnish with the cardamom.

Makes 1 drink

FIG SYRUP

Makes about 8 ounces

100 grams (3.5 ounces) dried figs, quartered (see Note)
½ cup sugar
½ cup hot water

Combine the figs, sugar, and hot water in a blender and blend until smooth. Strain through a fine-mesh sieve into an airtight container. Cover and refrigerate for up to 2 weeks.

Note: You'll be able to find dried figs year-round, but try this syrup with fresh figs during the summer when they are in season.

RYO PALMER

Haera Shin Foley, *Momofuku Noodle Bar, New York*

The Arnold Palmer, that timeless summer sip, is reimagined here with Asian influences. The matcha balances this tart, citrus-forward drink with herbaceous dryness, while also contributing a pretty ombré effect.

½ ounce yuzu juice
1 ounce fresh lemon juice
1 ounce Simple Syrup (1:1)
   (page 236)
2 ounces water
2 ounces chilled Matcha Tea
   (recipe follows)
1 lemon half-moon, for garnish
1 fresh mint sprig or fresh
   citrus leaf, for garnish

In a cocktail shaker, combine the yuzu juice, lemon juice, simple syrup, and water. Fill with ice and shake briskly. Strain into a chilled 12-ounce Collins glass filled with ice. Carefully pour the matcha tea on top to create an ombré effect. Garnish with the lemon and mint sprig.

Makes 1 drink

MATCHA TEA

Makes 2 cups

5.5 grams (0.2 ounce)
   Harney & Sons
   matcha powder
2 cups filtered water,
   at room temperature

In a jar, combine the matcha and water, cover with a lid, and shake vigorously until fully incorporated. Refrigerate for up to 48 hours.

FIZZY ALMOND

Erick Castro, *Raised by Wolves, San Diego*

As charming and effervescent as a debutante, Erick Castro's Fizzy Almond delivers sweet nuttiness and a delightful fizz. Fragrant with notes of marzipan, this is a very satisfying drink that you can throw together in just a matter of minutes.

1 ounce fresh lemon juice
1¹/2 ounces orgeat or almond syrup
Pebble ice
3 ounces chilled Fever-Tree
    club soda
1 fresh mint sprig, for garnish
3 or 4 whole roasted Marcona
    almonds, for garnish (optional)
1 fresh lemon wheel, for garnish
    (optional)

Combine the lemon juice and orgeat in a cocktail shaker. Add 1 ice cube and shake. Strain into a chilled 12-ounce Collins glass filled with pebble ice. Slowly top with the chilled club soda. Garnish with the mint spring and, if using, the Marcona almonds and lemon wheel.

Makes 1 drink

CARAJILLO VIRGEN

Irving Araico, *Rufino, Mexico City*

Think of the carajillo as the Mexican version of an Irish coffee, or as an Italian caffè corretto. In the boozy version, a carajillo combines coffee with a shot of spirit, such as Licor 43, brandy, or rum. In this aromatic drink, the heat from the fresh ginger adds texture to the soft vanilla and coffee notes.

2 thin slices fresh ginger, peeled
1/2 ounce Vanilla Syrup (page 237)
1 ounce high-quality cold brew coffee, chilled
Large ice cube
1 1/2 ounces chilled Sprite, for topping
Dash of ground coffee beans, for garnish

In a cocktail shaker, gently muddle the ginger with the vanilla syrup. Add the coffee, fill with ice, then shake briskly until frothy. Strain into a chilled 8-ounce rocks glass over a large ice cube. Slowly top with the Sprite to maintain the foam. Garnish with the ground coffee.

Makes 1 drink

EVERLEAF COOLER

Ryan Chetiyawardana, *Lyaness, London*

You don't always need a ton of ingredients to make a lively, flavorful drink if you focus on using a few high-quality options.

Everleaf is a gorgeous non-alcoholic aperitif built around botanicals such as vetiver, gentian, and saffron. Silver tip tea (also called silver needle tea and Yinzhen tea) is the most prized Chinese white tea. Gathered in early spring, silver tip tea is less processed than its counterparts, which means it's high in antioxidants.

The Everleaf Cooler starts with a honey nose, then follows through with a subtle spring-morning bouquet of orange blossom, vanilla, and hay.

1/2 ounce Everleaf non-alcoholic bittersweet aperitif (available at everleafdrinks.com and thewhiskyexchange.com)
3 1/2 ounces Cold-Brewed Rare Tea (recipe follows)
1 small cantaloupe slice, for garnish
1 fresh mint sprig, for garnish

In a chilled 12-ounce Collins glass, combine the Everleaf and tea. Fill with ice and stir gently. Garnish with the cantaloupe and mint sprig.

Makes 1 drink

COLD-BREWED RARE TEA

Makes about 7 ounces

5.5 grams (0.2 ounce) loose silver tip tea, such as from Rare Tea Company (available from Amazon)
7 ounces cold water

In a jar, combine the tea and water. Cover and let steep in the refrigerator for 6 hours. Strain the tea into an airtight container, cover, and refrigerate for up to 2 weeks.

GARD-EN-ING

Aaron Michael Siak, *Bibo Ergo Sum, Los Angeles*

Confident and animated, this is the cocktail version of the life of the party. With a touch of sweetness and a hint of savory linked by a citrus zing, this drink hits all the right notes.

1½ ounces Seedlip Garden 108 distilled non-alcoholic spirit (available at specialty stores and from Amazon)
¾ ounce fresh lime juice
¾ ounce Celery Syrup
(recipe follows)
¼ ounce Mint Stem Syrup
(recipe follows)
Chilled seltzer, for topping
1 lime wheel, for garnish

In a cocktail shaker, combine the Seedlip, lime juice, celery syrup, and mint stem syrup. Fill with ice and shake briskly. Strain into a chilled 12-ounce Collins glass filled with ice. Top with seltzer and garnish with the lime wheel.

Makes 1 drink

CELERY SYRUP

Makes 3¼ cups

2.5 grams (0.08 ounce) malic
  acid (available at specialty
  stores and from Amazon)
5 grams (1 teaspoon) sea salt
6 ounces water
500 grams (17.6 ounces) fresh
  celery, diced (see Note)
500 grams (17.6 ounces) sugar,
  or as needed

In a blender, combine the malic acid, salt, and water. Add the celery in batches and blend until smooth (or see Note for juicer instructions). Strain through cheesecloth or a fine muslin bag (such a nut milk bag) into a small bowl. Twist the cloth to squeeze out as much liquid as possible.

Measure the liquid by volume and pour it back into the blender. Add an equal volume of sugar. Blend until smooth. Pour into a bottle, cover, and refrigerate for up to 1 week.

Note: If you have a juicer, make 1½ cups fresh celery juice (from about 2 full celery hearts), then add the malic acid, salt, and water and shake well to combine. You'll still need to strain the liquid, but it will be less pulpy if you use juice.

MINT STEM SYRUP

Too often, we use only one part of a fruit or herb and discard the rest. This syrup makes use of mint stems, which are left over after the leaves have been pulled off for garnishes. (If you have leaves and no use for them, feel free to add them.)

Makes 3 cups

25 grams (0.9 ounce) fresh
  mint stems
500 grams (17.6 ounces)
  boiling water
500 grams (17.6 ounces) sugar,
  or as needed

In a medium heatproof bowl, combine the mint stems with the boiling water. Let steep for 30 minutes. Strain through a fine-mesh sieve. Weigh the liquid and add an equal weight of sugar. Stir until the sugar completely dissolves. Pour into bottles, cover, and refrigerate for up to 2 weeks.

TEA TONIC

David Paz, *Xaman, Mexico City*

The homemade sous vide pineapple tea in David Paz's Tea Tonic lends this drink a lilting, aromatic freshness. Delicate and fruity, this cocktail makes a perfect companion to spring parties and long summer nights.

2½ ounces Pineapple Tea
  (recipe follows)
Scant ¾ ounce agave nectar
½ ounce fresh lime juice
½ ounce egg white
Chilled Fever-Tree tonic water,
  for topping
1 lemon twist, for garnish
Edible flowers, such as pansies
  (available at specialty stores
  and chefs-garden.com),
  for garnish

In a cocktail shaker, combine the pineapple tea, agave, lime juice, and egg white; shake vigorously. Fill with ice and shake again until silky and frothy. Strain into a chilled 12-ounce Collins glass filled with ice. Top with tonic water. Squeeze the lemon twist over the drink, rub it around the rim of the glass, then discard. Garnish with edible flowers.

Makes 1 drink

SOUS VIDE PINEAPPLE TEA

David Paz's pineapple tea stands on its own as a fresh drink with a welcome acidic bite and no added sugars. Two pineapple peels are the minimum you should use, but if you have the peels from an entire pineapple, feel free to drop those into the sous vide bag. (The rest of the ingredients remain the same.) Be sure to clean them well before cooking. Keep the tea well chilled and enjoy on its own or paired with sparkling water.

Makes about 2 cups

2 pieces fresh pineapple
  peel, each at least
  2x2 inches
2½ cups water
5.5 grams (0.2 ounce)
  citric acid (available at
  specialty stores and
  from Amazon)

Using an immersion circulator, heat a water bath to 158°F (70°C). Combine the pineapple peel, water, and citric acid in a sous vide bag. Vacuum seal and submerge in the water bath for 1 hour. Remove the bag and plunge it into an ice bath. Snip off one corner of the bag and strain the syrup into an airtight container. Let fully cool, then cover and refrigerate for up to 2 weeks.

SO FRESH, SO CLEAN

Giovanni Allario, *Le Syndicat Cocktail Club, Paris*

This lush, floral French highball presents a bouquet of honey, citrus, and soft lavender against a crackle of spice. Memorable and winsome, this drink from Paris's famed Le Syndicat delivers a punch of flavor with minimal effort.

2 ounces **Lavender Verbena Cordial** (recipe follows)

2 ounces **high-quality spiced kombucha, such as cardamom or ginger**

2 teaspoons **fresh lemon juice**

Cracked ice

Dried food-grade rose petals or edible fresh flowers (available at specialty stores and chefs-garden.com), for garnish (optional)

Fresh lavender and lemon verbena (available at specialty stores and chefs-garden.com), for garnish (optional)

In a chilled 12-ounce Collins glass, combine the cordial, kombucha, and lemon juice. Fill the glass with cracked ice and stir to combine. Garnish with the rose petals or the fresh lavender and lemon verbena.

Makes 1 drink

LAVENDER VERBENA CORDIAL

Makes about 2 cups

2 cups **water**

5.5 grams (0.2 ounce) **dried lavender**

55 grams (0.2 ounce) **dried lemon verbena**

125 grams (4.4 ounces) **sugar**

5.5 grams (0.2 ounce) **citric acid** (available at specialty stores and from Amazon)

In an airtight container, combine the water, lavender, and lemon verbena. Cover and let infuse at room temperature for 1 day. Strain through a cheesecloth-lined fine-mesh sieve into a clean airtight container. Add the sugar and citric acid and stir until the sugar dissolves. Cover and refrigerate for up to 1 month.

THE NEO-NOIR

Elva Ramirez, *Brooklyn, New York*

The gimlet is one of those classic drinks that's ostensibly easy to make, yet simple to mess up if you don't have the right kick of lime. A straightforward mix of lime cordial and gin, a great gimlet doesn't pull any of its citrus punches.

In *The Long Goodbye*, Raymond Chandler wrote, "A real gimlet is half gin and half Rose's Lime Juice and nothing else." We've updated Chandler's gimlet to make it no-proof, but you should still feel free to sip this in a corner while moodily staring out a window.

2 ounces Ritual Zero Proof gin alternative (available at ritualzeroproof.com and from Amazon)
2 ounces Limeade Cordial (recipe follows)

In a cocktail shaker, combine the gin alternative and cordial. Fill with ice and shake briskly until well chilled and the ice is broken up. Strain into a chilled 6-ounce Nick and Nora glass.

Makes 1 drink

LIMEADE CORDIAL

This cordial came about as a way to use the fresh citrus peels I frequently had left over after juicing.

To make the cordial, you'll start with an oleo-saccharum ("oily sugar"), a sugar infused with the natural oils from the citrus peels. The longer it sits, the more flavor it takes on.

Consider this cordial recipe a starting point. Use the guidelines with a range of citrus peels (orange, lemon, grapefruit) to come up with your own cordials. Citric acid adds sourness but it's also a preservative, so it extends the life of your cordial. Be sure to use only very fresh citrus fruits.

Makes about 2/3 cup

2 limes
1/2 lemon
1/2 cup sugar
About 1/3 cup hot water
10 grams (0.35 ounce) citric acid (available at specialty stores and from Amazon)

Using a vegetable peeler or sharp knife, peel the limes and the lemon half, taking care to avoid the white pith. (Reserve the peeled fruit for another use.) Transfer the peels to an airtight container, add the sugar, and cover. Shake to coat the peels with the sugar. Let infuse at room temperature, shaking occasionally, for at least 24 hours or up to 48 hours, until the oil from the peels mixes with the sugar to make an infused syrup. Strain the syrup through a fine-mesh sieve into a liquid measuring cup, gently pressing on the peels to extract as much liquid as possible. Discard the peels.

Measure the syrup by volume, pour it into an airtight container, and add an equal volume of hot water. Stir to combine, add the citric acid, and stir again. Cover, and refrigerate for up to 1 month.

GT&C

Elva Ramirez, *Brooklyn, New York*

Of all the drinks in the spirits universe, I have to confess that the gin & tonic is my absolute true love. It's simple and refreshing, but surprisingly adaptable to the always evolving world of high-quality gins and tonics.

If you're looking for a way to indulge your G&T habit but keep it fresh and no-proof, check out my revamped version, the GT&C (gin, tonic & cordial).

2 ounces Ritual Zero Proof gin alternative (available at ritualzeroproof.com and from Amazon)

1 ounce Limeade Cordial (page 83)

1 (6.8-ounce) bottle Fever-Tree elderflower tonic water, chilled

In a chilled 12-ounce highball glass, combine the gin alternative and cordial. Fill with ice and stir to combine. Top with some of the tonic water and serve with the bottle on the side to top again, as desired.

Makes 1 drink

JASMINE COOLER

Meaghan Dorman, *Dear Irving Gramercy, New York*

Minty and vibrant, Meaghan Dorman's Jasmine Cooler has a touch of mojito vibes. The drink opens with a bite of mint, while jasmine syrup adds a wisp of floral dimension. Easy-drinking and approachable, this drink makes a lovely aperitif that will take you into the night hours.

4 or 5 fresh mint leaves
1½ ounces Jasmine Syrup
(recipe follows)
1½ ounces fresh lemon juice
Chilled Fever-Tree club soda,
for topping
1 lemon wheel, for garnish
1 fresh mint sprig, for garnish

In a cocktail shaker, combine the mint leaves, jasmine syrup, and lemon juice. Fill with ice and shake briskly. Strain into a chilled 12-ounce Collins glass filled with ice. Top with club soda. Garnish with the lemon wheel and mint sprig.

Makes 1 drink

JASMINE SYRUP

Lotus jasmine, or jasmine pearl, is a delicate high-quality green tea made from hand-rolled young tea leaves that are infused with night-blooming jasmine flowers.

The jasmine "pearls" are added to hot water; while steeping, the flower "blooms," opening into a lotus shape. Steep the tea for up to 5 minutes, or until the leaves have completely opened.

Makes about 3 ounces

¼ cup hot brewed
jasmine pearl green tea
2 ounces sugar

In a small bowl, combine the tea and sugar; stir until the sugar dissolves. Strain the syrup into an airtight container and let cool. Cover and refrigerate for up to 1 week.

NON-ALCOHOLIC
GIN & TONIC

The Clumsies bar team, *The Clumsies, Athens, Greece*

G&T lovers, rejoice. Gin's endearing qualities center around its punch of heady aromatics. None of that charm is lost in this homemade no-proof gin substitute, created by the stellar team at The Clumsies in Athens. A drink that opens with a fresh garden bouquet and ends with an astringent piquancy? Consider us smitten.

2 ounces Gin Hydrosol (page 172)
Chilled Fever-Tree Mediterranean tonic water, for topping
1 cucumber strip, skewered, for garnish
Pinch of freshly ground black pepper, for garnish

Fill a chilled 12-ounce Collins glass with ice. Add the gin hydrosol, then top with tonic water and stir. Garnish with the cucumber strip and pepper.

Makes 1 drink

BUBBLES FOR EVERYONE

Jeremy Le Blanche, *queensyard, New York*

Charming and effervescent, Jeremy Le Blanche's Bubbles for Everyone is an instant crowd-pleaser. A sweet, dark syrup leans into the homemade sparkling "wine," creating a confident drink designed to be the life of the party.

5 ounces Queensyard
    Alcohol-Free Sparkling Wine
    (recipe follows)
2 ounces Seedlip Grove 42
    distilled non-alcoholic spirit
    (available at specialty stores
    and from Amazon)
1 ounce Kola Nut Syrup
    (recipe follows)
1 orange twist, for garnish

In a mixing glass, combine the sparkling wine, Seedlip, and syrup. Fill with ice and stir to combine. Pour into a chilled Champagne flute. Squeeze the orange twist over the drink, rub it around the rim of the glass, then place it on the rim.

Makes 1 drink

KOLA NUT SYRUP

Tonka beans are prized by chefs and bakers for their intense vanilla and almond flavors. These beans are thought to be toxic in high quantities, so they may be hard to find. Kalustyan's in New York and some Amazon vendors sell them. You can substitute the same amount of coffee beans for a different profile that will still work.

Makes 16 ounces

2 cups (16 ounces) Coca-Cola
4 tonka beans
1 cup superfine sugar

In a small saucepan, combine the Coke and tonka beans. Pour the sugar in a little at a time, as it will cause the soda to bubble. Once all the sugar has been added, simmer over low heat, stirring occasionally, until you can taste the essence of the tonka beans in the syrup, about 30 minutes. Don't let the mixture boil.

Strain the syrup through a fine-mesh sieve into an airtight container. Let cool completely, then cover and refrigerate for up to 1 week.

QUEENSYARD ALCOHOL-FREE SPARKLING WINE

Making a convincing sparkling wine has to do with texture as well as the just-so layering of acidity, sweetness, and brightness. With not too much effort, this is a great stand-in for fun bubbles.

Makes about 16 ounces

1/2 cup chilled filtered apple juice
10 grams (0.35 ounce) loose peach herbal tea (see Note)
1 1/2 cups chilled verjus blanc, such as Wölffer Estate (see Note)

In a liquid measuring cup, combine the apple juice with the peach tea. Let steep for 1 hour. Strain into a pitcher and discard the tea leaves. Add the verjus and stir to combine.

Working in batches, if necessary, carbonate with a Soda-Stream or other home carbonation machine. Transfer to a bottle, cap tightly, and refrigerate for up to 1 week.

Note: One thing to keep in mind: Many peach teas, such as Bigelow's Perfect Peach herbal tea, feature flowers, such as hibiscus, that will impact the color of your infusion. A hibiscus-tinted peach tea is certainly lovely and won't hurt the final drink, but if you'd prefer a yellow shade, first scan the back of your tea package and make sure it doesn't include ingredients that may give the sparkling wine a color other than peach.

Verjus is the juice of unripe grapes. Because it's still a somewhat new category in the U.S., quality from new brands can range from excellent to funky. Look for verjus made by established wine companies, such as New York's Wölffer Estate.

HALF DAY

Meaghan Dorman, *Dear Irving Gramercy, New York*

Margarita fans, this one is for you. Fresh citrus and earthy jalapeños lean into floral sweetness and vegetal tang in this juicy drink.

3 cucumber wheels
3 ounces Wölffer Estate verjus blanc (see Note)
3/4 ounce Jalapeño-Infused Agave Syrup (page 160)
1/2 ounce fresh lime juice
Large ice cube
1 cucumber wheel, for garnish

In a cocktail shaker, gently muddle 3 cucumber wheels. Add the verjus, jalapeño syrup, and lime juice. Fill with ice and shake briskly. Strain over a large ice cube into a chilled 10-ounce double rocks glass. Garnish with the remaining cucumber wheel floating on the ice.

Makes 1 drink

Note: Verjus is the juice of unripe grapes. Because it's still a somewhat new category in the U.S., quality from new brands can range from excellent to funky. Look for verjus made by established wine companies, such as New York's Wölffer Estate.

GINGER AND MINT SWIZZLE

Maxime Belfand, *Saxon + Parole, New York*

Piquant and cheerful, this spicy drink yields to a soft ginger flourish and closes with a kick of cayenne. Expect guests to ask for a second round.

2 ounces chilled brewed Bellocq No. 48, Pic du Midi tea (mint, black currant leaf, and ginger tea; available at bellocqtea.com)
2 ounces Cayenne Apple Cider (recipe follows)
½ ounce 2:1 Agave Syrup (page 237)
½ ounces fresh lemon juice
Crushed ice (see page 16)
1 pickled ginger slice, rolled, for garnish
1 fresh mint sprig, for garnish

In a chilled 12-ounce Collins glass, combine the tea, cider, agave syrup, and lemon juice. Fill with crushed ice and stir briskly. Top with more ice, if needed, then garnish with the pickled ginger and mint sprig.

Makes 1 drink

CAYENNE APPLE CIDER

Makes 8 ounces

1 cup apple cider
¼ teaspoon cayenne pepper

Combine the cider and cayenne in a bottle, cover, and shake to combine. Refrigerate for up to 2 weeks.

OFF THE 10

Elva Ramirez, *Brooklyn, New York*

For many decades, non-alcoholic beers were watery, stilted, and had few fans. But as the zero-proof movement expands into craft brewing, expect a new range of flavorful no- and low-proof options to emerge. Case in point: the very charming no-proof Mango Cart by Golden Road, a wheat beer inspired by Los Angeles fruit sellers. (Golden Road makes a boozy Mango Cart as well.)

Italy's Venice has its famous Bellini, which mixes peach puree and prosecco. In a nod to Southern California's Venice (which is just off the I-10 highway), we combine fresh mango puree, kumquat-infused Seedlip, verjus, and chilled non-alcoholic beer to make a drink that's delightfully dry, citrus-forward, and full of chill L.A. vibes.

1 cup halved kumquats

2 ounces Seedlip Grove 42 distilled non-alcoholic spirit (available at specialty stores and from Amazon)

2 ounces fresh mango puree

1 ounce Wölffer Estate verjus blanc (see Note)

1 (12-ounce) can chilled Golden Road Mango Cart non-alcoholic wheat brew beer

In a mixing glass, combine the kumquats and Seedlip and let infuse for at least 1 hour, but ideally overnight. Strain the kumquat-infused Seedlip into a cocktail shaker. Add the mango puree and verjus. Fill with ice and shake well to combine. Strain into a chilled Spanish-style goblet or Burgundy wineglass filled with ice. Slowly top with the beer and add more ice if needed. Serve with the remaining beer on the side.

Makes 1 drink

Note: Verjus is the juice of unripe grapes. Because it's still a somewhat new category in the U.S., quality from new brands can range from excellent to funky. Look for verjus made by established wine companies, such as New York's Wölffer Estate.

CRYPTO CURRENCY

Elva Ramirez, *Brooklyn, New York*

The Gold Rush is one of my favorite cocktails, invented at Sasha Petraske's famed Milk & Honey bar and now served all over the world. Basically a cold toddy, it's a shaken drink with bourbon, fresh lemon, and honey. In my no-proof update, we're combining Ritual Zero Proof's whiskey alternative with honey, lemon, and a zing of ginger for a crackling finish.

Given that the original is named after the Gold Rush, my version nods to today's monetary Wild West: Meet the Crypto Currency.

2¹/2 ounces Ritual Zero Proof
    whiskey alternative
    (available at ritualzeroproof.com
    and from Amazon)
³/4 ounce Honey Syrup (1:1)
    (page 236)
³/4 ounce fresh lemon juice
¹/2 teaspoon Ginger Syrup
    (page 238)
Large ice cube
Small cube of honeycomb,
    for garnish
Fresh ginger slices, for garnish

In a cocktail shaker, combine the whiskey alternative, honey syrup, lemon juice, and ginger syrup. Fill with ice and shake briskly until well chilled. Strain into a chilled 8-ounce rocks glass over a large ice cube. Garnish with the cube of honeycomb and a fresh slice of ginger.

Makes 1 drink

PAMPLEMOUSSE

Camille Vidal, *La Maison Wellness, London*

Camille Vidal's Pamplemousse is a classy Mediterranean-style gin & tonic, made all the more elegant by being no-proof. Camille's custom grapefruit-rose-rosemary honey brings gin's aromatics to mind, while London Essence tonic's delicate tones close out the experience with a crisp, dry finish.

1 ounce plus 2 teaspoons non-alcoholic gin, such as Ritual Zero Proof gin alternative (available at ritualzeroproof.com and from Amazon) or Ceder's non-alcoholic alt-gin (available at the thewhiskyexchange.com)

Scant ¾ ounce fresh lime juice

Scant ¾ ounce Rosemary, Rose, and Grapefruit Honey (recipe follows)

London Essence Co. grapefruit and rosemary tonic water (available from Amazon), for topping

1 fresh rosemary sprig, for garnish

1 grapefruit half-moon, for garnish

In a chilled 12-ounce double rocks glass, combine the non-alcoholic gin, lime juice, and honey. Fill with ice and stir briskly. Top with the tonic and garnish with the rosemary sprig and grapefruit.

Makes 1 drink

ROSEMARY, ROSE, AND GRAPEFRUIT HONEY

Makes about 16 ounces

8 ounces high-quality honey

8 ounces hot water

Holy Lama rosemary extract spice drops (available at holylama.co.uk) or other high-quality rosemary extract, to taste

Holy Lama rose extract spice drops (available at holylama.co.uk) or other high-quality rose extract, to taste

2 drops high-quality grapefruit essential oil

Combine the honey and hot water in a jar. Stir until the honey dissolves. Add 1 or 2 drops of each of the spice drops and the grapefruit oil. Stir and taste. Add more spice drops, as desired. Let cool to room temperature. Cover and refrigerate for up to 1 week.

SPICED TEASE

Aaron Michael Siak, *Bibo Ergo Sum, Los Angeles*

This crowd-pleasing drink will remind you of a grown-up Arnold Palmer with layered citrus notes and a delicious mint flare that pleasantly lingers after each sip. Perfect for summer afternoons, or cool winter weekends when you want to bring the sunshine inside.

1½ ounces Seedlip Spice 94 distilled non-alcoholic spirit (available at specialty stores and from Amazon)
1¼ ounces Citrus Cordial (recipe follows)
¼ ounce Ginger Syrup (page 238)
¼ ounce fresh lemon juice
Chilled Moroccan Mint Green Tea (recipe follows), **for topping**
1 lemon wheel, for garnish

In a cocktail shaker, combine the Seedlip, cordial, ginger syrup, and lemon juice. Fill with ice and shake briskly. Strain into a chilled 12-ounce Collins glass filled with ice. Top with the tea and garnish with the lemon wheel.

Makes 1 drink

CITRUS CORDIAL

This citrus cordial can be made with any combination of citrus fruits, such as grapefruit, lemons, and limes. Use the recipe as a template and adapt it as you like, as long as you start with equal parts water to peels, and add equal parts where noted.

Makes about 4½ ounces

6 ounces water
6 ounces lemon peels, no pith (from about 3 medium lemons)
2 ounces fresh lemon juice (from about 3 medium lemons), or as needed
85 grams (3 ounces) sugar
⅛ teaspoon citric acid (available at specialty stores and from Amazon), or to taste
¼ teaspoon malic acid (available at specialty stores and from Amazon), or to taste

In a small saucepan, bring the water to a boil. Add the lemon peels, cover, and boil for 5 minutes. Strain the citrus stock through a chinois or fine-mesh sieve into a small heatproof bowl, gently pressing on the peels to extract as much liquid as possible. Discard the peels.

Return the citrus stock to the saucepan and gently simmer until it's reduced by a third, 2 to 4 minutes.

Weigh the citrus stock, then add an equal weight of lemon juice. Combine well, then weigh again and add an equal weight of the sugar (about 3 ounces).

Ideally, you will measure the volume in ml, then add 0.25 percent citric acid in grams and 0.50 percent malic acid in grams, and adjust sugar levels as needed. Think of a sweet lemonade flavor. Alternatively, you can work slowly and gradually add the citric acid (increasing by ⅛ teaspoon at a time) and the malic acid (increasing by ¼ teaspoon at a time) to the mixture, stirring and tasting as you add them.

MOROCCAN MINT GREEN TEA

Moroccan mint green tea, also called Maghreb mint tea, is a particular blend of green tea and spearmint (and occasionally other flavors such as lemongrass). Traditionally prepared with fresh spearmint, you can find pre-mixed tea at retailers such as Trader Joe's.

Makes about 16 ounces

1 teaspoon loose Moroccan mint green tea (or about 3 tea bags)
16 ounces water

In a liquid measuring cup, combine the tea and water and infuse overnight at room temperature. Strain through a coffee filter or fine-mesh sieve and discard the solids. Pour into a bottle, cover, and refrigerate for up to 3 days.

BOBBY JONES

Daniel Sabo, *Lumière Brasserie at the Fairmont Century Plaza, Century City*

Bobby Jones was the celebrated golfer who founded the Masters Tournament. There is a boozy cocktail that also bears his name, but in a nod to the famed Arnold Palmer drink, the namesake of another golfing legend, here is a full-bodied and feisty no-proof drink that packs several strong flavors into a small package.. Look for zesty citrus, a spark of mint, and the textured dryness of black tea.

2 ounces strong-brewed black tea, chilled
1 ounce Acid-Adjusted Grapefruit Juice (recipe follows)
½ ounce Rich Simple Syrup (2:1) (page 236)
5 fresh mint leaves
1 lime wheel, for garnish

In a cocktail shaker, combine the tea, grapefruit juice, simple syrup, and mint. Fill with ice and shake vigorously. Strain into a chilled 10-ounce rocks glass filled with ice. Garnish with the lime wheel and serve.

Makes 1 drink

ACID-ADJUSTED GRAPEFRUIT JUICE

Acid-adjusting citrus, in this case grapefruit, means tweaking the acidity so that it matches that of lime juice. This allows you to make a more balanced drink.

Makes about 4 ounces

4 ounces fresh pink grapefruit juice
5 grams (0.18 ounce) citric acid (available at specialty stores and from Amazon)

Whisk together the juice and citric acid in a small bowl until combined. Transfer to an airtight glass container, cover, and refrigerate for up to 2 weeks.

CELEBRATION SPRITZ

Elva Ramirez, *Brooklyn, New York*

This drink pays homage to the timeless charm of an Aperol spritz, with a savory-bitter cordial dancing over brisk bubbles. Start with equal parts but, as the Spanish do, feel free to top with more fizz to extend the drink.

2 ounces **Grapefruit Tarragon Cordial** (recipe follows)
2 ounces chilled **Wölffer Estate Petite Rosé verjus** (see Note)
1 (12-ounce) bottle **Casamara Club Sparkling Amaro Onda soft drink**, chilled

Fill a cocktail shaker with ice, add the cordial, and shake briskly. Pour into a chilled Spanish-style goblet or Burgundy wineglass filled with ice. Slowly pour in the verjus and 2 ounces of the amaro soft drink. Stir once and add more ice, if needed. Serve with the bottle of amaro soft drink on the side.

Makes 1 drink

Note: Verjus is the juice of unripe grapes. Because it's still a somewhat new category in the U.S., quality from new brands can range from excellent to funky. Look for verjus made by established wine companies, such as New York's Wölffer Estate.

GRAPEFRUIT TARRAGON CORDIAL

Grapefruit's sweet notes make it one of my favorite fruits, but I'm also quite partial to its inherent bitterness. When combined with tarragon, the citrus gains savory depths.

Makes 18 ounces

2 grapefruits, peeled, seeded, and cut into small chunks
4 ounces Seedlip Grove 42 distilled non-alcoholic spirit (available at specialty stores and from Amazon)
8 ounces water
14 grams (0.5 ounce) fresh tarragon
255 grams (9 ounces) sugar

In a medium saucepan, combine the grapefruit and Seedlip. Cover and cook over low heat until the grapefruit falls apart without caramelizing, about 1 hour.

Bring the water to a boil in a small saucepan. Remove from the heat, add the tarragon, and let infuse for 30 minutes. Strain through a fine-mesh sieve into the grapefruit mixture. Cover and simmer over low heat for about 15 minutes. By now, the mixture will resemble a pulpy soup. Cover and let cool completely.

Strain through a fine-mesh sieve into a clean small saucepan. Add the sugar and cook gently over low heat until it dissolves, 2 to 3 minutes. Let cool completely and refrigerate for up to 2 weeks.

SKY HOOK

Sam Johnson, *Death & Co, New York*

The Sky Hook opens with the exuberance of fresh green apples, follows up with a halo of vanilla, and ends with a kick of citrus charm. Neither overly sugary nor mouth-puckering sour, this drink sits on the just-so balance of sweet-meets-tart.

1½ ounces fresh green apple juice
½ ounce fresh lemon juice
½ ounce fresh lime juice
½ ounce yuzu juice
¾ ounce Vanilla Syrup (page 237)
¾ ounce Honey Syrup (1:1)
   (page 236)
5 to 10 fresh tarragon leaves
Crushed ice (see page 16)
1 apple fan, for garnish

In a cocktail shaker, combine the apple juice, lemon juice, lime juice, yuzu juice, vanilla syrup, honey syrup, and tarragon. Fill with ice, shake briskly, then fine-strain into a chilled 12-ounce tulip glass (see Note) filled with crushed ice. Garnish with the apple fan planted in the ice, just inside the rim of the glass. Serve with a straw.

Makes 1 drink

Note: *Tulip glasses have wide bottoms and flared rims, and are traditionally used to serve beer, such as Belgian ales.*

TEMPEST

Robert Hiddleston and Mia Johansson, *Bar Swift, London*

Bar Swift is one of London's most dynamic bars, serving up stellar hospitality alongside inventive takes on classics. Their homemade sherbets shine in several of their drinks, including the non-alcoholic Tempest, which is a sprightly dance of delicate citrus and floral accents.

3¹/2 ounces chilled high-quality
   kombucha
2 teaspoons elderflower cordial,
   such as Belvoir Farms
2 teaspoons Honey Syrup (2:1)
   (page 236)
2 teaspoons Lemon Sherbet
   (recipe follows)
2 dashes Bittermens Boston Bittahs
   (available at bittermens.com and
   from Amazon)
1 dash Fee Brothers celery bitters
   (available at feebrothers.com
   and from Amazon)
1 long grapefruit twist, for garnish

In a mixing glass, combine the kombucha, elderflower cordial, honey syrup, sherbet, and both bitters. Add ice and stir briskly. Strain into a chilled coupe. Squeeze the grapefruit twist over the drink, rub it around the rim of the glass, then drop it in.

Makes 1 drink

Note: Kombucha and Bittermens bitters have trace amounts of alcohol.

LEMON SHERBET

Makes about 1¹/2 cups

4 lemons
1 cup superfine sugar,
   or as needed

Peel all the lemons, avoiding the pith, and set the peels aside in a large bowl. Juice the lemons and measure the juice by volume. Then measure out an equal volume of sugar (1 cup juice and 1 cup sugar, for example).

Add the sugar to the bowl with the peels, tossing them with your hands to coat, and let sit for at least 1 hour. Stir in the lemon juice until incorporated, then strain into an airtight container, gently pressing on the solids to extract all the liquid. Cover and freeze for up to 1 month.

FRUITY & FLORAL

NATASHA

Pippa Guy, *American Bar at The Savoy, London*

The American Bar at the Savoy has been at the forefront of sophisticated no-proof drinks for many years, in part because they have an international clientele, but also because, as one of the world's most lauded bars, they bring an innovative approach to every drink they make.

Several drinks in this book feature different takes on hibiscus. That's because, in addition to its lipstick-worthy red color, hibiscus imparts tart, almost citrus notes as well as a soft, floral bouquet.

Pippa Guy's Natasha is a well-rounded drink with citrus, spice, floral, fruity, and nutty notes. It opens up as you sip it, and is the kind of long drink that pairs well with spicy foods, like barbecue.

1³/4 ounces Seedlip Grove 42 distilled non-alcoholic spirit (available at specialty stores and from Amazon)

1¹/2 ounces chilled Hibiscus Water (recipe follows)

1 ounce fresh pink grapefruit juice

¹/2 ounce grenadine

2 teaspoons fresh lime juice

2 drops almond essence or almond extract

Chilled Fever-Tree premium Indian tonic water, for topping

1 fresh mint sprig, such as baby pineapple mint (available at specialty stores and chefs-garden.com), for garnish (optional)

In a cocktail shaker, combine the Seedlip, hibiscus water, grapefruit juice, grenadine, lime juice, and almond essence. Fill with ice and shake well. Strain into a chilled pint glass or other 16-ounce glass filled with ice. Top with the tonic and garnish with the mint sprig.

Makes 1 drink

HIBISCUS WATER

Using whole, dried hibiscus flowers, not a hibiscus tea, is key to getting the strongest flavor for this water, which is meant to showcase the sour bite as well as the vibrant reds that these flowers produce.

Makes about 12 ounces

2 cups water
56 grams (6 ounces)
   dried hibiscus flowers
Small pinch of citric acid
   (available at specialty
   stores and from Amazon)

In a small saucepan, bring the water to a boil. Remove from the heat, add the hibiscus, and let steep for at least 15 minutes or up to 30 minutes. Add the citric acid and stir well to combine. Strain the hibiscus water into an airtight container, let cool completely, then cover and refrigerate for up to 4 days.

CHILD'S PLAY

Sean Quinn, *Death & Co, Denver*

What does nostalgia taste like? You'll find the answer in the Child's Play from Death & Co Denver's Sean Quinn. Sweetly reminiscent of a Creamsicle, with orange and vanilla top notes and a lingering caramel finish, this drink unfurls a new flavor with each sip.

The cream soda syrup, made with August Uncommon's Psychocandy tea, makes up the backbone of this drink. It's important to use this particular blend. Bonus: It's a delicious, very original tea blend and you'll have some left over.

1¹/2 ounces Sous Vide Psychocandy Cream Soda Syrup (recipe follows)

1¹/2 ounces Acid-Adjusted Orange Juice (recipe follows)

4 ounces chilled Fever-Tree club soda, for topping

1 whole or half-dried orange wheel, for garnish

In a cocktail shaker, combine the syrup and orange juice. Fill with ice and shake well. Strain into a chilled 12-ounce Collins glass filled with ice. Top with the club soda and garnish with the orange wheel.

Makes 1 drink

SOUS VIDE PSYCHOCANDY CREAM SODA SYRUP

Makes about 12 ounces

500 grams (17.6 ounces)
    cane sugar
500 grams (17.6 ounces) water
11 grams (0.4 ounce) pure
    vanilla extract
0.6 gram (0.02 ounce)
    cream of tartar
25 grams (0.9 ounce) loose
    August Uncommon
    Psychocandy tea
    (darkly sweet rooibos with
    pumpkin and caramel;
    available at august.la)

In a medium saucepan, combine the sugar, water, vanilla, and cream of tartar. Cook over low heat, whisking occasionally to prevent burning, until the mixture reaches 215°F (101°C), 25 to 30 minutes.

Using an immersion circulator, heat a water bath to 135°F (57°C).

Remove the sugar syrup from the heat. Transfer it to a sous vide bag and add the tea. Vacuum seal and submerge the water bath set at 135°F (57°C) for 2 hours. Remove the bag and plunge it into an ice bath. Snip off one corner of the bag and strain the syrup into an airtight container. Cover and refrigerate for up to 1 week.

ACID-ADJUSTED ORANGE JUICE

Acid-adjusting sounds intimidating but it's really just about bringing up the acidity of juice (in this case, orange) to match that of lemon or lime. A more sour juice is sometimes desired when balancing a drink to avoid overwhelming it with sweetness.

On average, one orange will yield 2 ounces of juice. To get 17 ounces of juice, you'll need 8 to 9 medium oranges.

Makes about 16 ounces

500 grams (17.5 ounces) fresh
    orange juice
1 gram (¼ teaspoon) malic acid
    (available at specialty stores
    and from Amazon)
5 grams (1 teaspoon) citric acid
    (available at specialty stores
    and from Amazon)

Combine the orange juice, malic acid, and citric acid in a medium bowl. Whisk until well combined. Transfer to an airtight container, cover, and refrigerate for up to 1 week.

POMEGRANATE PHOSPHATE

Erick Castro, *Raised by Wolves, San Diego*

Soda fountains in the late nineteenth century were one of the earliest places to get well-made no-proof drinks. This easy-to-make drink, from San Diego's lauded Raised by Wolves, is an addictive mix of sweetness and fizzy bubbles balanced against a hint of acidity.

2 ounces grenadine
10 grams (2 teaspoons) acid
    phosphate (see Note)
Pebble ice
4 ounces chilled Fever-Tree
    club soda
1 lime wheel, for garnish
1 brandied cherry, for garnish

In a pint glass, combine the grenadine and acid phosphate. Fill with pebble ice and stir lightly. Top with the club soda, then garnish with the lime wheel and brandied cherry.

Makes 1 drink

Note: Acid phosphate is a combination of phosphoric acid and phosphate mineral salts. It enhances the sour character of drinks without the citrus tang. You can find it on Amazon.

ZEN GARDEN

Camille Vidal, *La Maison Wellness, London*

Floral and delicate, Camille Vidal's Zen Garden opens up like a perfume. The soft peach and jasmine flavors in the London Essence soda sparkle against the green notes of Seedlip Garden 108.

1 ounce plus 2 teaspoons Seedlip Garden 108 distilled non-alcoholic spirit (available at specialty stores and from Amazon)

½ ounce chilled brewed green tea

5 ounces chilled London Essence Co. white peach and jasmine soda (available at thewhiskyexchange.com), for topping

1 cucumber wheel, for garnish

1 edible jasmine flower (available at specialty stores and chefs-garden.com), for garnish

Combine the Seedlip and tea in a chilled 12-ounce Collins glass. Fill with ice and stir briskly. Top with the soda and garnish with the cucumber wheel and jasmine flower.

Makes 1 drink

HIBISCUS TEA

Irving Araico, *Rufino, Mexico City*

Silky and fruity, with a compelling chocolate top note, this drink, courtesy of Mexico City's Rufino, has a satisfying pucker and a lingering dry finish.

1½ ounces chilled brewed hibiscus tea
2 ounces fresh pineapple juice
½ ounce Simple Syrup (1:1) (page 236)
Large ice cube
1 dehydrated pineapple wheel, for garnish
Freshly grated bittersweet chocolate, for garnish

In a cocktail shaker, combine the hibiscus tea, pineapple juice, and simple syrup. Fill with ice and shake briskly, then strain into an 8-ounce rocks glass over a large ice cube. Garnish with the pineapple wheel and dust the top with a fresh grating of bittersweet chocolate.

Makes 1 drink

GROVE & TONIC

Jeremy Le Blanche, *queensyard, New York*

Rose layers on top of rosemary; peach amplifies grapefruit: Jeremy Le Blanche's Grove & Tonic is bursting summer freshness. Infusing Seedlip with peach herbal tea introduces several expressive aromas, while pink-tinted ice cubes make this a head-turning cocktail.

3 ounces Seedlip Grove 42 distilled non-alcoholic spirit (available at specialty stores and from Amazon)
2 peach herbal tea bags (see Notes)
Rose Ice Cubes (recipe follows), for serving
Chilled London Essence Co. grapefruit and rosemary tonic water (available from Amazon), for topping
1 fresh mint sprig, for garnish (see Notes)

In a liquid measuring cup, combine the Seedlip with the tea bags and let steep for 1 hour. Remove and discard the tea bags. Pour the tea into a chilled 12-ounce highball glass and fill the glass with the rose ice cubes. Top with the tonic water and garnish with the mint sprig.

Makes 1 drink

Notes: A happy accident occurred while testing this drink. I discovered that many peach teas, such as Bigelow's Perfect peach tea, feature flowers, such as hibiscus, which will impact the color of your infusion. A pink hue won't hurt your drink, and in this case, the pink liquid plus rose-infused ice cubes play off each other. If you'd prefer a clear, more "gin"-like appearance, scan the ingredients in your peach tea for those that will change the color of the tea.

This drink is garnished with mint, but there are many varieties of mint, including flowering mint, that can jazz up your drinks for parties. Look for mint varieties at specialty stores and chefs-garden.com.

ROSE ICE CUBES

Yield varies on ice cube molds

3 cups cold spring water
5 grams (¼ cup) dried food-grade rose petals (just petals, not buds)

In a medium bowl, combine the water and rose petals and let steep overnight. Strain the rose water through a fine-mesh sieve into a pitcher; discard the rose petals. Pour into ice cube molds (see Note) and freeze until completely solid, at least 3 hours.

Note: Using larger molds will result in cubes that last longer in drinks.

EVERBEE

Paul Mathew, *Everleaf Drinks, London*

Paul Mathew is a conservation biologist, which informs not just his approach to creating his non-alcoholic aperitif, Everleaf, but also his custom drinks. "We've seen a lot about the importance of bees as ecosystem pollinators," he says. "This drink is a celebration of the part bees play in making sure Everleaf's plants are around forever."

Bee pollen gives the Everbee a dense nuttiness that filters the honey into an element that's more than merely sweet. The drink is well-rounded and polished with a refined floral dryness.

1½ ounces Everleaf non-alcoholic bittersweet aperitif (available at everleafdrinks.com and thewhiskyexchange.com)
Generous ¾ ounce Honey, Lemon, and Bee Pollen Cordial (recipe follows)
Generous ¾ ounce chilled verjus (preferably crab apple or grape verjus; see Note)
Bee pollen, for garnish
1 small honeycomb cube, for garnish

In a cocktail shaker, combine the Everleaf, cordial, and verjus and shake. Strain into a chilled 6-ounce Nick and Nora glass. Garnish with a dusting of bee pollen and serve with the cube of honeycomb on the side.

Makes 1 drink

Note: Verjus is the juice of unripe grapes. Because it's still a somewhat new category in the U.S., quality from new brands can range from excellent to funky. Look for verjus made by established wine companies, such as New York's Wölffer Estate.

HONEY, LEMON, AND BEE POLLEN CORDIAL

Makes about 8 ounces

6 grams (0.2 ounce) bee pollen
5 ounces water
1 strip of lemon peel, with pith
5 ounces high-quality honey
4 grams (0.14 ounce) malic acid (available at specialty stores and from Amazon)

Lightly toast the bee pollen in a small saucepan to release its aromas, about 1 minute. Add the water, lemon peel, honey, and malic acid and bring to a simmer over low heat, then cook without boiling for 8 to 10 minutes. Set aside to fully cool, then strain and refrigerate for up to 2 weeks.

SPRING NETTLE SOUR

Paul Mathew, *Everleaf Drinks, London*

Gardeners will probably be familiar with stinging nettles, a weed that gets its name from the sharp fibers coating its surface, which irritate anything unlucky enough to brush up against them. Nettles have been brewed into teas for centuries, and you'll probably find their flavor comfortingly familiar.

Nettles have a pretty sour taste that's not quite floral, yet not entirely citric. The Spring Nettle Sour opens up with a bouquet of honeyed sweetness and finishes on a gratifying bitter note.

1½ ounces Everleaf non-alcoholic bittersweet aperitif (available at everleafdrinks.com and thewhiskyexchange.com)
Generous ¾ ounce Nettle Cordial (recipe follows)
½ ounce fresh lemon juice
½ ounce egg white or aquafaba (liquid from canned chickpeas)
Splash of chilled Fever-Tree club soda
1 edible flower, such as anise hyssop (available at specialty stores and chefs-garden.com), for garnish (optional)

In a cocktail shaker, combine the Everleaf, cordial, lemon juice, and egg white; shake vigorously. Fill with ice and shake again. Add the club soda to the shaker, then double strain (through a fine-mesh strainer, as well as the shaker's own strainer) into a chilled 8-ounce rocks glass filled with ice. Garnish with the flower.

Makes 1 drink

NETTLE CORDIAL

Makes about 10 ounces

250 grams (8.8 ounces) sugar
1 cup water
28 grams (1 ounce) dried stinging nettle leaves (see Note)
14 grams (0.5 ounce) citric acid (available at specialty stores and from Amazon)

Combine the sugar, water, nettle leaves, and citric acid in a medium saucepan. Bring to a gentle simmer, stirring to dissolve the sugar. Remove from the heat, cover, and let sit at room temperature overnight. Strain through a fine-mesh sieve, transfer to a bottle, cover, and refrigerate for up to 2 weeks.

Note: Freshly picked nettles might be hard to come by, but if you have them, you can substitute 3.5 ounces freshly picked nettle tops for the dried flowers. Wear gloves while handling fresh nettles.

JULIET'S BALCONY

Elva Ramirez, *Brooklyn, New York*

The Garibaldi, a classic Italian aperitivo, is a study in minimalism. I first fell in love with the Garibaldi at Dante in New York, where they perfected the just-so combination of Campari and "fluffy" freshly squeezed orange juice. When I arrived in Verona for the first time, this was the drink I ordered to sip while watching couples stroll past on the piazza.

In this homage, three excellent no-proof products are combined to mimic Campari's signature bitterness. Everleaf adds texture and a float of vanilla, while the Seedlip Grove 42 punches up the vibrant citrus. Casamara Club's Alta soda finishes the drink with gorgeous Italian chinotto, baking spices, and just a touch of sparkle. Freshly squeezed orange juice is a must.

2½ ounces fresh orange juice
1 ounce Everleaf non-alcoholic
   bittersweet aperitif
   (available at everleafdrinks.com
   and thewhiskyexchange.com)
1 ounce Seedlip Grove 42 distilled
   non-alcoholic spirit
   (available at specialty stores
   and from Amazon)
¾ ounce chilled Casamara Club
   Sparkling Amaro Alta soft drink
1 orange twist, for garnish

In a cocktail shaker, combine the orange juice, Everleaf, and Seedlip. Fill with ice and shake briskly, then strain into a chilled 6-ounce Nick and Nora glass. Slowly top with the Alta. Garnish with the orange twist.

Makes 1 drink

TALK TO HER

Lynnette Marrero, *Speed Rack cofounder, Llama Inn, New York*

Spice-forward with a pineapple backbone, this is the drink to serve during daytime gatherings that turn into languid afternoons. Inspired by a sangria, the Talk to Her will definitely spark chatter and crushes.

1¹/2 ounces Seedlip Spice 94 distilled non-alcoholic spirit (available at specialty stores and from Amazon)
2 ounces chilled Wölffer Estate Petite Rosé verjus
³/4 ounce fresh pineapple juice
¹/2 ounce Cinnamon Syrup (page 237)
1 pineapple leaf, for garnish

In a mixing glass, combine the Seedlip, verjus, pineapple juice, and cinnamon syrup. Fill with ice and stir briskly. Pour into a wineglass filled with ice. Garnish with the pineapple leaf.

Makes 1 drink

TALK TO HER PUNCH BOWL

Makes 6 to 8 servings
(1 large punch bowl)

10 ounces Seedlip Spice 94 distilled non-alcoholic spirit (available at specialty stores and from Amazon)
13 ounces chilled Wölffer Estate Petite Rosé verjus (see Note)
5 ounces fresh pineapple juice
3¹/2 ounces Cinnamon Syrup (page 237)

In a large punch bowl, combine the Seedlip, verjus, pineapple juice, and cinnamon syrup. Fill with ice and stir briskly. Ladle into wineglasses filled with ice.

Note: To keep punches cold, make oversized ice cubes by freezing water in large plastic containers. Large ice blocks will melt slower.
Note: Verjus is the juice of unripe grapes. Because it's still a somewhat new category in the U.S., quality from new brands can range from excellent to funky. Look for verjus made by established wine companies, such as New York's Wölffer Estate.

SHE PRETTY

Eamon Rockey, *Listen Bar, New York*

If there's a vanguard to the American no-proof movement, you'll find it at Listen Bar, where grown-up non-alcoholic drinks by star bartenders are served in a party atmosphere. The debut drinks program was overseen by Eamon Rockey, who crafted drinks at Eleven Madison Park and Betony.

One look at this drink and you'll see where it gets its name. The She Pretty will remind you of a grown-up strawberry shortcake, made with wild berries at the height of their freshness. That's not to say it's cloying or childish, but rather light, dry, and tart.

2½ ounces Strawberry Consommé
  (recipe follows)
1 ounce fresh lemon juice
1 large egg white
3 drops rose water
1 edible flower, such as Egyptian
  star flower blossom
  (available at specialty stores and
  chefs-garden.com), for garnish

In a cocktail shaker, combine the consommé, lemon juice, egg white, and rose water. Shake vigorously to emulsify, then fill with ice and shake again. Double strain (through a fine-mesh strainer, as well as the shaker's own strainer) into a chilled 8-ounce coupe and garnish with the flower.

Makes 1 drink

STRAWBERRY CONSOMMÉ

Makes about 28 ounces

1 pound strawberries, hulled
  and quartered
3 cups water
½ cup sugar

In a medium saucepan, combine the strawberries and water and bring to a simmer, about 4 minutes. Remove from the heat, cover, and let steep until the strawberries have lost their color and the liquid is bright red, about 30 minutes. Strain the consommé into a large bowl, stir in the sugar, and let cool slightly. Transfer to an airtight container and let cool completely. Cover and refrigerate for up to 5 days.

Note: The consommé really captures the essence of the strawberries. If you have any left over, consider making your own strawberry soda by stirring together ½ cup consommé, 1½ cups chilled sparkling water, and 3 dashes of acid phosphate.

SWASHBUCKLE

Daniel Sabo, *Lumière Brasserie at the Fairmont Century Plaza, Century City*

Light and fruity to start, with a slight dryness at the end, the Swashbuckle is a winsome drink wrapped in a caress of orange blossom.

2 cucumber wheels
½ ounce Agave Syrup (1:1)
   (page 237)
3 ounces fresh pineapple juice
1 ounce fresh lime juice
2 dashes orange blossom water
1 fresh cilantro sprig or 1 cape gooseberry, for garnish (optional)

In a cocktail shaker, gently muddle the cucumber with the agave syrup. Add the pineapple juice, lime juice, and orange blossom water. Fill with ice and shake vigorously. Strain into a chilled 10-ounce double rocks glass filled with ice. Garnish with the cilantro sprig or cape gooseberry and serve.

Makes 1 drink

ALPENGLOW

Tyson Buhler, *Death & Co, Denver*

The satisfying fizz of a homemade soda meets the sour charm of hibiscus in Tyson Buhler's Alpenglow. Neither cloying nor very dry, the Alpenglow sits at the intersection of bubbles, sweetness, and citrus accents.

2½ ounces Sous Vide Alpenglow Cordial (recipe follows)
½ ounce fresh lime juice
2 ounces chilled Perrier lemon-flavored sparkling mineral water
1 fresh bay leaf, for garnish
1 young beet stalk or sunset beet blush leaves (available at specialty stores and chefs-garden.com), for garnish (optional)

Combine the cordial and lime juice in a mixing tin with a few ice cubes. Shake briefly, then strain into a chilled 12-ounce Collins glass filled with ice. Stir in the mineral water and garnish with the bay leaf and beet stalk.

Makes 1 drink

SOUS VIDE ALPENGLOW CORDIAL

Makes 32 ounces

35.3 ounces Simple Syrup (1:1) (page 236)
25 grams (0.9 ounce) dried Jamaican red sorrel (hibiscus)
5 grams (0.18 ounce) lactic acid (available at specialty stores and from Amazon)
5 grams (0.18 ounce) fresh bay leaf
5 grams (0.18 ounce) loose Assam black tea

Using an immersion circulator, heat a water bath to 135ºF (57ºC). Combine the simple syrup, red sorrel, lactic acid, bay leaf, and tea in a sous vide bag. Vacuum seal and submerge in the water bath for 2 hours. Remove the bag and plunge it into an ice bath. Once fully cool, snip off one corner of the bag and strain the syrup into an airtight container. Cover and refrigerate for up to 2 weeks.

SOBER CURIOUS

Natasha David and Jeremy Oertel, *Hotel Kinsley, New York*

With just a flick of the wrist, the Sober Curious transforms a few everyday ingredients into a sprightly drink with a surprising tart back note, a sumptuous pink hue, and an enchanting sweetness. If you love Clover Clubs, this is your new vibe.

1¹/2 ounces fresh lemon juice
1 ounce Simple Syrup (1:1)
   (page 236)
³/4 ounce grenadine
¹/2 teaspoon apple cider vinegar
1 large egg white
1¹/2 ounces chilled seltzer,
   for topping
1 dehydrated lemon wheel,
   for garnish

In a cocktail shaker, combine the lemon juice, simple syrup, grenadine, vinegar, and egg white. Shake vigorously until frothy. Fill with ice and shake vigorously again. Strain into a chilled 6-ounce coupe glass. Slowly pour the seltzer in the center of the drink to maintain the froth. Garnish with the lemon wheel.

Makes 1 drink

SCARLET AND SPICE

Meaghan Dorman, *Raines Law Room, New York*

Consider the Scarlet and Spice, with its balance of sweet, tart, and spicy notes, a well-rounded drink companion. Have it alone or let it shine alongside flavor-packed fare like a cheeseburger or hot wings.

4 ounces chilled brewed In Pursuit of Tea Scarlet Glow herbal tea (available at inpursuitoftea.com) or other high-quality hibiscus tea

3/4 ounce fresh lemon juice

1/2 ounce Cinnamon Syrup (page 237)

1 orange wheel, for garnish

In a cocktail shaker, combine the tea, lemon juice, and cinnamon syrup. Fill with ice and shake briskly. Strain into a chilled 12-ounce Collins glass filled with ice and garnish with the orange wheel.

Makes 1 drink

COFFEE LEAF

Paul Mathew, *Everleaf Drinks, London*

The espresso martini is a cocktail classic because of its sweet-bitter-floral trifecta. Paul Mathew's Coffee Leaf unfurls a banner of crisp aromatic flavors in every single sip. You'll never miss the vodka.

Generous ¾ ounce Everleaf non-alcoholic bittersweet aperitif (available at everleafdrinks.com and thewhiskyexchange.com)
Generous ¾ ounce strong cold-brew coffee, such as Jot Ultra Coffee
Generous ¾ ounce Cascara Syrup (recipe follows)
3 coffee beans, for garnish

In a cocktail shaker, combine the Everleaf, coffee, and cascara syrup. Fill with ice and shake vigorously to break up the ice and create a nice froth. Strain into a chilled 6-ounce Nick and Nora glass and garnish with the coffee beans.

Makes 1 drink

CASCARA SYRUP

Cascara (Spanish for "shell" or "husk") is the dried red flesh of the coffee fruit, and is typically thrown away during coffee production. Also sold as "coffee cherry" or "coffee fruit," cascara is reputed to be high in antioxidants and can be enjoyed on its own as a floral, fruity hot tea. This syrup makes a spectacular addition to your morning coffee.

Makes about 6 ounces

200 grams (7 ounces) unrefined brown sugar (such as raw, turbinado, Demerara, or muscavado sugar)
6.75 ounces water
28 grams (1 ounce) cascara (available at specialty coffee roasters and from Amazon)

In a small saucepan, combine the brown sugar, water, and cascara and stir over medium heat until the sugar dissolves. Bring to a boil, then reduce the heat and simmer, stirring occasionally, for 10 minutes. Remove from the heat and let cool to room temperature. Strain through a fine-mesh sieve, transfer to a bottle, cover, and refrigerate for up to 2 weeks.

SGT. PEPPER'S LONELY HEARTS CLUB

Mariena Mercer, *The Cosmopolitan of Las Vegas*

It's no hyperbole to say that Mariena Mercer is behind the most-talked-about drinks in Las Vegas. Ever since she debuted as chef mixologist at The Cosmopolitan in 2010, her popular drinks have minted millions in revenue for the resort (over $75 million in beverage sales in 2018 alone).

Her culinary-inflected cocktails always pack a surprise layer, as evidenced in the delectable strawberry-peppercorn shrub that forms the basis of this drink. Opening with a flick of lavender bubbles and chewy berries lifted by a soft white cranberry backdrop, this is a sweet drink with pleasant depths.

2 ounces Pink Peppercorn
  Lychee Strawberry Shrub
  (recipe follows)
2 ounces chilled white cranberry
  juice
Crushed ice (see page 16)
Chilled lavender soda
  (such as DRY), for topping
1 edible orchid (available at
  specialty stores and
  chefs-garden.com), for garnish

In a cocktail shaker, combine the shrub and cranberry juice. Fill with ice cubes and shake briskly, then strain into a chilled 10-ounce rocks glass filled with crushed ice. Top with lavender soda and garnish with the orchid.

Makes 1 drink

PINK PEPPERCORN LYCHEE STRAWBERRY SHRUB

Makes about 16 ounces

16 ounces Simple Syrup (1:1)
  (page 237)
16 ounces strawberry puree
225 grams (8 ounces) canned
  lychee in syrup, pureed
  until smooth
28 grams (1 ounce)
  pink peppercorns
28 grams (1 ounce)
  red wine vinegar

Combine the simple syrup, strawberry puree, lychee puree, peppercorns, and vinegar in a medium sauce-pan. Heat over medium heat for 20 minutes. Remove from the heat and let cool completely. Strain through a fine-mesh sieve into an airtight container, then cover and refrigerate for up to 1 month.

FLIP THE SWITCH

Natasha David, *Nitecap, New York*

There are a lot of flavors packed into this drink, from concentrated strawberry to a spike of serrano pepper heat to the soft warmth of cinnamon. They all fold into each other in a drink that resembles a debonair strawberry soda. Seltzer is key to lengthening the drink and giving it fizz, but be careful not to pour so much that you overwhelm its key flavors.

1¹/2 ounces Strawberry Serrano Pepper Shrub (recipe follows)
³/4 ounce fresh pineapple juice
¹/2 ounce fresh lemon juice
¹/2 ounce Sous Vide Cinnamon Syrup (page 221)
Chilled seltzer, for topping
1 pineapple slice, for garnish
1 serrano pepper slice, for garnish (optional)
1 strawberry, for garnish (optional)

In a cocktail shaker, combine the shrub, pineapple juice, lemon juice, and cinnamon syrup. Fill with ice and shake briskly. Strain into a chilled 10-ounce Collins glass filled with ice. Slowly top with cold seltzer, a little at time, so as not to mute the drink's flavors. Garnish with the pineapple slice and, if using, the serrano pepper slice and strawberry.

Makes 1 drink

STRAWBERRY SERRANO PEPPER SHRUB

Bright red, sweet, and with a definite kick of heat, this shrub reminds me of a spicy Jolly Rancher in the best possible way.

Makes about 24 ounces

16 ounces apple cider vinegar
225 grams (8 ounces) strawberries, hulled and chopped
1 serrano chile, halved lengthwise
7 grams (0.25 ounce) fresh cilantro
About 2 cups sugar

Combine the vinegar, strawberries, chile, and cilantro in an airtight container, cover, and let sit at room temperature for 3 days. Strain through a fine-mesh sieve; discard the solids.

Measure the volume of the liquid, then pour it into a medium saucepan. Add an equal volume of sugar and simmer until the sugar is dissolved. Let cool to room temperature, then transfer to an airtight container. Cover and refrigeratefor up to 3 months.

VEGETAL & SAVORY

GARDEN SOUR

Victoria Canty, *The Fat Radish, New York*

Savory drinks can also be light and frothy. Consider Victoria Canty's Garden Sour, which punches up the vegetal notes in Seedlip Garden 108 with a zing of green apple, lemon, and celery.

Aquafaba, the liquid in canned chickpeas, works like an egg white. You'll want to first dry shake the drink to emulsify and get the liquid frothy, then add ice and shake again.

1½ ounces Seedlip Garden 108 herbal distilled non-alcoholic spirit (available at specialty stores and from Amazon)
½ ounce aquafaba (liquid from canned chickpeas)
½ ounce Simple Syrup (1:1) (page 236)
1½ ounces Green Juice Mix (recipe follows)
Large pinch of nigella seeds, for garnish
Small bunch of celery leaves, for garnish

In a cocktail shaker, combine the Seedlip, aquafaba, simple syrup, and green juice and shake vigorously until frothy. Fill with ice and shake again until fluffy. Double strain (through a fine-mesh strainer, as well as the shaker's own strainer) into a chilled 6-ounce coupe and garnish with the nigella seeds.

Gently gather the celery leaves and chiffonade (cut into small ribbons), then sprinkle them on top of the nigella seeds.

Makes 1 drink

GREEN JUICE MIX

This lively juice recipe can be halved if you like, but you can easily find a way to use the green juice as a base for a morning drink or post-workout pick-me-up. It is sour, so you'll have to add your own sweeteners: Try it with a dash of mint syrup or lightly sweetened, chilled mint tea.

Makes about 32 ounces

10 ounces fresh lemon juice
10 ounces fresh celery juice
12 ounces fresh green apple juice

After you have juiced all the produce and measured out the juices, filter them through a fine-mesh sieve to remote any sediment and pulp. Combine in a bottle, cover, and refrigerate for up to 4 days.

SEEDLIP SPICE AND ALL THINGS NICE

Aidan Bowie, *The Aviary, New York*

Aidan Bowie's Seedlip Spice and All Things Nice will be divisive because it's savory and spiked with an unmissable punch of curry. Bowie's drink is a great showcase of how no-proof drinks can borrow from culinary palates to create something fresh and audacious.

Vadouvan, a French curry spice blend, forms the backbone of this drink, which is strikingly complex. It's meant to be lingered over, in the same way you might take your time enjoying a Negroni. It will also open up and change as the ice melts.

2 ounces chilled Coconut Oolong Tea (recipe follows)

1¹/2 ounces Seedlip Spice 94 distilled non-alcoholic spirit (available at specialty stores and from Amazon)

¹/2 ounce verjus blanc (see Note)

¹/2 ounce Sous Vide French Curry Syrup (recipe follows)

¹/2 ounce Simple Syrup (1:1) (page 236)

1 citrus wheel, dried or fresh, for garnish

In a chilled 12-ounce Collins glass, combine the tea, Seedlip, verjus, curry syrup, and simple syrup. Fill with ice and stir briskly. Top with more ice. Garnish with the citrus wheel.

Makes 1 drink

Note: Verjus is the juice of unripe grapes. Because it's still a somewhat new category in the U.S., quality from new brands can range from excellent to funky. Look for verjus made by established wine companies, such as New York's Wölffer Estate.

SOUS VIDE FRENCH CURRY SYRUP

Makes about 4 ounces

20 grams (0.7 ounce) vadouvan
(a French curry-like spice
blend; available at specialty
stores and from Amazon)

10 grams (0.35 ounce) black
cardamom pods, cracked
open

7 ounces Simple Syrup (1:1)
(page 236)

In a spice blender, combine the vadouvan and carda-mom; blitz until well-combined. Transfer to a medium bowl and stir in the simple syrup. Transfer to a sous vide bag. Vacuum seal and submerge in a sous vide bath set at 140°F (60°C) for 1 hour. Remove the bag and plunge in an ice bath. Snip off one corner and strain the syrup into an airtight container. Cover and refrigerate for up to 2 weeks.

COCONUT OOLONG TEA

Makes about 20 ounces

50 grams (1.8 ounces)
Freak of Nature oolong
tea leaves (available
at rareteacellar.com)

25 grams (0.9 ounce)
unsweetened coconut
flakes, toasted

25 grams (0.9 ounce) shredded
fresh coconut

4 cups boiling water

In a medium heatproof bowl, combine the tea with the toasted and fresh coconut. Add the boiling water and let steep for 6 minutes. Strain the tea into a jar and let cool completely. Cover and refrigerate for up to 4 days.

Note: You will have a lot of tea leaves left over after one steep. Rather than tossing the tea leaves after one use, you can re-steep them with 2 cups boiling water for 6 minutes up to two more times. Strain the tea and let cool completely. Blend the steeped teas together and refrigerate for up to 4 days. (If you make the extra tea batch, use the blended version in your cocktail for a little more nuance.)

Enjoy as a fragrant morning or afternoon tea. Consider adding a teaspoon or two of Cinnamon Syrup (page 237) or Vanilla Turmeric Syrup (page 203), and a splash of oat milk; it might become your new breakfast ritual.

NO MAMES MARIA

Lynnette Marrero, *Speed Rack co-founder, Llama Inn, New York*

Brunch is often synonymous with drinking alcohol, but it doesn't have to be. Lynnette Marrero's non-alcoholic take on the Bloody Mary packs an earthy, juicy punch without any of the guilt.

1¹/2 ounces Seedlip Grove 42 distilled non-alcoholic spirit (available at specialty stores and from Amazon)

3 ounces Morris Kitchen Tomato Beet Bloody Mary mixer (available at morriskitchen.com and from Amazon)

1 lime wheel, for garnish

In a mixing glass, combine the Seedlip and Bloody Mary mixer. Fill with ice and stir briskly. Pour into a chilled wineglass. Top with ice, if necessary. Garnish with the lime wheel.

Makes 1 drink

MORNING GROVE FIZZ

Ryan Chetiyawardana, *Lyaness, London*

Created in the style of morning pick-me-ups, this fizz is a decadent swirl of herbaceous and garden-fresh flavors jostling against an earthy, silky backdrop.

1 tarragon sprig
½ ounce Simple Syrup (1:1)
　(page 236)
1 ounce Seedlip Grove 42 distilled
　non-alcoholic spirit
　(available at specialty stores
　and from Amazon)
1 teaspoon Seedlip Garden 108
　distilled non-alcoholic spirit
　(available at specialty stores
　and from Amazon)
1¾ ounces chilled green tea
　kombucha (see Note)
½ ounce fresh lime juice
Scant ¾ ounce double cream
　or heavy cream
Generous ¾ ounce egg white
1½ ounces chilled Fever-Tree
　club soda, for topping
1 fresh lime twist or tarragon sprig,
　for garnish

In a cocktail shaker, muddle the tarragon with the simple syrup. Add the Seedlip Grove, Seedlip Garden, kombucha, lime juice, cream, and egg white. Wrap a tea towel around the shaker, then shake to emulsify. The bubbles in the kombucha will build pressure; open gently.

Fill with shaker with ice, then wrap again with the towel and shake again. Double strain (through a fine-mesh strainer, as well as the shaker's own strainer) into a chilled 9-ounce sling glass or other tall glass. Slowly top with club soda to maintain the froth, then garnish with the lime twist or tarragon sprig.

Makes 1 drink

Note: Kombucha has trace amounts of alcohol.

BETTER AVE. WINE

Eamon Rockey, *Betony, New York*

In his beet wine, Eamon Rockey aims to replicate the tannins and body of red wine. (The drink's name is a pun on the French word for beets, *betterave*.) In this very easy non-alcoholic "wine," chioggia beets' earthy tones melt into the fresh acidity of the green apples. Strong-brewed oolong tea, which has tobacco and leather notes, provides the backdrop. Drink it with a slight chill.

18 ounces (2¼ cups) fresh green apple juice
8 ounces (1 cup) fresh chiogga beet juice
16 ounces (2 cups) strong-brewed oolong tea, chilled

Chill the apple juice and beet juice in separate containers overnight to allow any sediment and foam to settle. Skim off the foam from each. Filter the juices through a fine-mesh sieve into a large container, leaving behind any sediment. Stir in the tea until well combined. Transfer to two wine bottles and chill lightly (to about 50°F/10°C) before pouring into red wine glasses. Keep refrigerated for up to 1 week.

Makes 8 servings (about 5½ cups)

ALMOST FAMOUS

Lynnette Marrero, *Speed Rack cofounder, Llama Inn, New York*

Bright and fruity, this sangria-inspired drink is a charming addition to any brunch or daytime occasion. If you're looking for a party-friendly recipe, make the drink in a punch bowl (see recipe at right) and let guests serve themselves.

2 ounces chilled verjus blanc
(see Note)

1½ ounces Seedlip Garden 108 distilled non-alcoholic spirit (available at specialty stores and from Amazon)

¾ ounce fresh pink grapefruit juice, strained through a fine-mesh sieve

½ ounce Celery Syrup
(recipe follows)

Celery leaves, for garnish

In a mixing glass, combine the verjus, Seedlip, grapefruit juice, and celery syrup. Fill with ice and stir briskly. Pour into a wineglass. Top with ice, if necessary. Garnish with celery leaves.

Makes 1 drink

Note: Verjus is the juice of unripe grapes. Because it's still a somewhat new category in the U.S., quality from new brands can range from excellent to funky. Look for verjus made by established wine companies, such as New York's Wölffer Estate.

ALMOST FAMOUS PUNCH BOWL

Makes about 8 servings
(1 punch bowl)

13 ounces verjus blanc
(see Note)
10 ounces Seedlip Garden 108
distilled non-alcoholic spirit
(available at specialty stores
and from Amazon)
5 ounces pink grapefruit juice,
strained through a fine-
mesh sieve
3¹/2 ounces Celery Syrup
(recipe follows)
Large block of ice (see Note)
Celery leaves, for garnish

In a punch bowl, combine the verjus, Seedlip, grape-fruit juice, and celery syrup with the block of ice (see Note). Stir to combine. Serve in chilled wineglasses filled with ice cubes. Garnish with celery leaves.

Note: When making a punch, freeze water in a big plastic container to create a large block of ice that will keep the punch cold but melt slowly.

CELERY SYRUP

Makes 12 ounces

1 cup fresh celery juice
1 cup sugar

Combine the celery juice and sugar in a Vitamix or other high-powered blender and blend until the sugar is dissolved. Strain through a fine-mesh sieve to remove any particles, then pour into a bottle. Cover and refrigerate for up to 2 weeks.

WHARNCLIFFE

Peder Schweigert, *Marvel Bar, Minneapolis*

When the acclaimed Marvel Bar went all in on a four-month exploration on dry drinks in 2020, this was on the menu. "I like the way the drink evolves as the ice melts," Marvel's beverage director Peder Schweigert says. "It starts almost a little too intense, and becomes balanced as the water is incorporated."

This sparkplug of a drink opens with a zippy zing of vinegar, then it's tempered by a vegetal sweetness and Ritual's gin-referencing botanicals.

2 ounces Ritual Zero Proof
    gin alternative (available at
    ritualzeroproof.com)
1 ounce Simple Syrup (1:1) (page 236)
1/2 ounce Homemade Pickle Brine
    (recipe follows) or brine
    from a jar of store-bought dill
    or spicy pickles
1 ounce fresh lime juice
2 cornichons, for garnish

In a mixing glass, combine the gin, simple syrup, pickle brine, and lime juice. Fill with ice and stir briskly. Pour into an ice-filled 10-ounce rocks glass. Halve the cornichons lengthwise, pierce with a skewer, and balance on the glass.

Makes 1 drink

HOMEMADE PICKLE BRINE

Marvel Bar makes their own pickle brine, which is detailed below. Peder Schweigert says you can use store-bought pickle brine, if you like. He likes a sweeter brine for the drink, but dill brines and spicy brines will work well.

    This brine, by the way, will wow you if you make it. You'll have plenty left over; vinegar is a preservative so it will last a long time. Add the brine to fresh cucumber or celery juice or mix it into a high-quality Bloody Mary mix for a sharp, vegetal, and deliciously savory sip.

Makes about 40 ounces

8 1/2 ounces cucumber juice
    (from 2 to 3 cucumbers)
17 ounces apple cider vinegar
9 ounces filtered water
35 grams (1.2 ounces)
    kosher salt
200 grams (6.75 ounces) sugar

Strain the cucumber juice into a blender. Add the remaining ingredients and blend on low speed until the sugar dissolves. Pour into a bottle, cover, and refrigerate for up to 4 months.

THIS SICK BEET

Jose Alejandro Ibanez, *Employees Only, New York City*

Beets often show up in non-alcoholic drinks because they impart an earthy complexity and, when shaken, give drinks a sturdy eye-catching froth. The beet and rosemary syrup from Employees Only in New York carries this drink with a savory base and lush, herbal aromatics.

1 ounce pomegranate juice
¾ ounce fresh grapefruit juice
¾ ounce fresh lemon juice
½ ounce Cinnamon Syrup
   (page 237)
¼ ounce Beet and Rosemary Syrup
   (recipe follows)
1 large egg white
1 dash Angostura bitters (see Note)
1 lemon twist, for serving
1 dehydrated lemon wheel,
   for garnish

In a cocktail shaker, combine the pomegranate juice, grapefruit juice, lemon juice, cinnamon syrup, beet and rosemary syrup, egg white, and bitters and shake vigorously. Fill the shaker with ice and shake again. Double strain (through a fine-mesh strainer, as well as the shaker's own strainer) into a chilled 7-ounce coupe. Squeeze the lemon twist over the drink, rub it around the rim of the glass, then discard. Garnish with the dehydrated lemon wheel.

Makes 1 drink

Note: The bitters in this drink have a trace amount of alcohol.

BEET AND ROSEMARY SYRUP

Makes about 9 ounces

6 ounces fresh beet juice
170 grams (6 ounces) sugar
2 fresh rosemary sprigs, tied in
   a bundle with kitchen twine

In a small saucepan, combine the beet juice and sugar. Tie the rosemary bundle to the handle of the saucepan with enough twine to submerge the bundle. Cook over low heat (without boiling), stirring occasionally, until the sugar dissolves completely, 5 to 7 minutes.

   Remove from the heat and let cool completely. Strain through a fine-mesh sieve into an airtight container. Cover and refrigerate for up to 1 week.

BELLE OF THE BALL

Jim Kearns, *The Happiest Hour, New York City*

The red bell peppers are unmissable in this cocktail, which is one of the most popular options at Manhattan's Happiest Hour. Between the Hellfire shrub and the syrup, you'll find a spectrum of pepper flavors, ending in a savory, vegetal finish.

2 ounces Sous Vide Red Bell
 Pepper Syrup (recipe follows)
1½ ounces fresh lemon juice
4 dashes Bittermens Hellfire
 Habanero shrub (available
 at bittermens.com and from
 Amazon; see Note)
Chilled Fever-Tree club soda,
 for topping
1 red bell pepper spear, for garnish

In a cocktail shaker, combine the red pepper syrup, lemon juice, and shrub. Fill with ice and shake briskly. Strain into a chilled highball glass filled with ice. Top with club soda and garnish with the bell pepper spear.

Makes 1 drink

Note: The Bittermens shrub has a trace amount of alcohol.

SOUS VIDE RED BELL PEPPER SYRUP

A good rule of thumb is, if you wouldn't eat it, it won't be good in a syrup. It's important to use fresh ingredients at all times.

Makes 8 ounces

225 grams (8 ounces)
 red bell peppers,
 stemmed and seeded
225 grams (8 ounces) sugar

Pulse the peppers in a food processor just until they form a coarse paste (not pureed smooth). Transfer to a large bowl; stir in the sugar and let sit at room temperature, stirring occasionally, until a syrup forms, about 1 day. (Alternatively, using an immersion circulator, heat a water bath to 140ºF/60ºC. Place the peppers and sugar in a sous vide bag. Vacuum seal and submerge in the water bath for 6 hours. Remove the bag and plunge it into an ice bath.)

Strain through a chinois or fine-mesh sieve into an airtight container, pressing on the solids to extract as much liquid as possible. Cover and refrigerate for up to 4 weeks.

DOUBLE GREEN

Meaghan Dorman, *Raines Law Room, New York*

Crisp and astringent, make the Double Green your summer zero-proof companion. It offers up a bracing vegetal note with a pleasant jalapeño burn that can be savored alone or paired with flavorful dishes like barbecue and burgers.

2 ounces fresh cucumber juice
¾ ounce Jalapeño-Infused Agave
    Syrup (recipe follows)
½ ounce fresh lemon juice
Chilled Fever-Tree club soda,
    for topping
2 or 3 cucumber wheels or ribbons,
    for garnish

In a cocktail shaker, combine the cucumber juice, jalapeño syrup, and lemon juice. Fill with ice and shake briskly. Strain into a chilled 12-ounce Collins glass filled with ice, top with club soda, and garnish with the cucumber wheels or ribbons.

Makes 1 drink

JALAPEÑO-INFUSED AGAVE SYRUP

Makes about 8 ounces

5 jalapeños, plus more
    if necessary, halved
    lengthwise
4 ounces water
4 ounces agave nectar

In a medium bowl, gently press the jalapeños with a wooden spoon to release some of the juices and seeds. Don't muddle too much or you will end up with too many floaty bits.

    Bring the water to a simmer in a medium saucepan. Remove from the heat and add the jalapeños and any accumulated juices. Let steep for 10 minutes.

    Add the agave and stir until combined. Let sit for another 10 minutes. This syrup should be spicy enough to make your lips tingle. If the syrup isn't spicy, add more jalapeños and steep for a few minutes more, tasting along the way so that it doesn't turn bitter.

    Strain the syrup into an airtight container, cover, and refrigerate for up to 1 month.

WHO ARE YOU CALLIN' FIDDLEHEAD?

Christine Wiseman, *Broken Shaker at the Freehand, Los Angeles*

Shrubs are a mixture of fruit or vegetables, sugar, and vinegar; they date back centuries as a way to preserve food. People who aren't fans of vinegar are sometimes put off by shrubs, because of the strong, tangy nose. That said, even the vinegar-averse crowd will fall for Christine Wiseman's shrub, which is made with marjoram, snap peas, and sherry vinegar, one of the softest expressions in the vinegar family.

Light and crisp yet also delightfully savory, this drink opens with a striking vegetal nose that's followed by an appealing minerality and a whisper of acid in the finish.

2 ounces Seedlip Garden 108 distilled non-alcoholic spirit (available at specialty stores and from Amazon)

1 ounce Snap Pea, Marjoram, and Pink Pepper Shrub (recipe follows)

2 dashes Fee Brothers celery bitters (available at feebrothers.com and from Amazon)

Crushed ice (see page 16)

Chilled coconut water, for topping

Edible flowers and pea tendrils (available at specialty stores and chefs-garden.com), for garnish

In a cocktail shaker, combine the Seedlip, shrub, and bitters. Fill with ice and shake well. Strain into a chilled 12-ounce Collins glass filled with crushed ice, top with coconut water, and garnish with the flowers and pea tendrils.

Makes 1 drink

SNAP PEA, MARJORAM, AND PINK PEPPER SHRUB

Makes about 16 ounces

10 to 15 fresh sugar snap peas
8 ounces (1 cup) sherry vinegar
8 ounces (1 cup) water
8 ounces (1 cup or 225 grams)
    sugar
14 grams (0.5 ounce) crushed
    pink peppercorns
7 grams (0.25 ounce)
    dried marjoram leaves

In a medium bowl, gently break open the snap peas to release their flavor, then add the remaining ingredients. Whisk until the sugar dissolves. Cover and let sit at room temperature for 48 hours. Strain through a fine-mesh sieve to remove all particles. Transfer to an airtight container, cover, and refrigerate for up to 1 month.

MEDINA NIGHT

Sam Johnson, *Death & Co, New York*

Don't let the garden-fresh ingredients fool you. Delicate and vibrant, the Medina Night is designed to encourage long, slow sips. Look for a spike of ginger and the lingering minerality of fresh carrots in the finish.

1½ ounces fresh carrot juice
1 ounce fresh lemon juice
¾ ounce water
¾ ounce Ginger Syrup (page 238)
½ ounce fresh orange juice
½ ounce Honey Syrup (1:1)
   (page 236)
Large ice cube

In a cocktail shaker, combine the carrot juice, lemon juice, water, ginger syrup, orange juice, and honey syrup. Fill with ice and and shake. Strain into a chilled 10-ounce double rocks glass over a large ice cube.

Makes 1 drink

PASSEGGIATA

Louis Lebaillif, *Little Red Door, Paris*

Little Red Door is one of Paris's most innovative bars, and this drink demonstrates why. Bittersweet no-proof drinks are the hardest to pull off, yet this drink unfurls a tapestry of flavors. The non-alcoholic amaro is made using a custom blend of four different infusions, each of which adds a different dimension of flavor. Think of it as making four separate teas that are then combined into a master mix.

A "passeggiata," by the way, is the Italian art of the leisurely evening stroll; it typically takes place between 5 p.m. and 8 p.m., when Italians meander outdoors and socialize before nightfall. Complex, bitter, and deeply layered, the drinkable Passeggiata will have you lingering over it as you make dinner plans with new friends.

2¹⁄₃ ounces Non-Alcoholic Amaro (recipe follows)

4 teaspoons Seedlip Grove 42 distilled non-alcoholic spirit (available at specialty stores and from Amazon)

1³⁄₄ ounces Fever-Tree club soda, chilled

2 orange twists, for garnish

In a chilled 10-ounce highball glass, combine the amaro, Seedlip, and club soda. Fill with ice and stir briskly. Squeeze one of the orange twists over the drink, rub it around the rim of the glass, then discard. Garnish with the remaining orange twist.

Makes 1 drink

NON-ALCOHOLIC AMARO

To make Little Red Door's amaro, you'll first create four different infusions, which are then combined. While there are a lot of ingredients, the infusions do the hard work for you, as there is no cooking required.

The vegetable glycerin in the final blend works as a sweetener and also a preservative. Once glycerin is added, this blend will stay fresh for up to 3 months in the fridge or up to a year in the freezer.

All the ingredients listed below can be found at Kalustyan's (foodsofnations.com).

Makes about 28 ounces

10.7 ounces Bitter Blend
 (recipe follows)
8.3 ounces Sweet Blend
 (recipe follows)
1 ounce plus 1 teaspoon Spice
 Blend (recipe follows)
1/2 ounce plus 1/2 teaspoon
 Floral Blend (recipe follows)
10 1/2 ounces vegetable glycerin
 (available at craft stores and
 from Amazon)
2 grams (0.07 ounce)
 tartaric acid
 (an organic souring agent)

In a large bowl, combine the bitter, sweet, spice, and floral blends. Add the glycerin and tartaric acid and stir until they dissolve. Pour the amaro into bottles or jars, cover, and refrigerate for up to 3 months.

BITTER BLEND

Makes about 12 ounces

30 grams (1 ounce)
 coffee beans
5 grams (0.18 ounce)
 gentian root
14 ounces water

Grind the coffee beans in a mortar and pestle or spice grinder. Transfer to a sous vide bag or a mason jar, add the gentian root, and seal tightly. Infuse at room temperature for 24 hours. Strain through a cheese-cloth-lined fine-mesh sieve into a clean jar, cover, and refrigerate for up to 3 weeks.

SWEET BLEND

Makes about 12 ounces

25 grams (0.9 ounce)
    cacao beans
2 vanilla beans, split and
    seeds scraped
14 ounces water

Grind the cacao beans in a mortar and pestle or spice grinder. Transfer to a sous vide bag or a mason jar, add the vanilla beans and water, and seal tightly. Let infuse at room temperature for 24 hours. Strain through a cheesecloth-lined fine-mesh sieve into a clean jar, cover, and refrigerate for up to 3 weeks.

SPICE BLEND

Makes about 12 ounces

15 grams (0.5 ounce)
    dried juniper berries
2 green cardamom pods
14 ounces water

Place the juniper berries in a sous vide bag or mason jar and gently bruise them; add the cardamom pods and water and seal. Let infuse at room temperature for 24 hours. Strain through a cheesecloth-lined fine-mesh sieve into a clean jar, cover, and refrigerate for up to 3 weeks.

FLORAL BLEND

Makes about 6 ounces

15 grams (0.5 ounce)
    dried chamomile flowers
10 grams (0.4 ounce)
    dried hops flowers
5 grams (0.18 ounce)
    dried lemon thyme
14 ounces water

Combine the chamomile flowers, hops flowers, lemon thyme, and water in a sous vide bag or a mason jar and seal tightly. Let infuse at room temperature for 24 hours. Strain through a cheesecloth-lined fine-mesh sieve, gently pushing on the solids, into a clean jar. Cover and refrigerate for up to 3 weeks.

NON-ALCOHOLIC NEGRONI

The Clumsies bar team, *The Clumsies, Athens, Greece*

A non-alcoholic Negroni is the vanguard of the no-proof space. Because the original is a showcase of gin's floral astringency, Campari's signature bitterness, and sweet vermouth's complexity, re-creating that flavor profile without alcohol is a challenge.

Enter the globally lauded bar team at Athens's The Clumsies, who are famous for making their own brews. This recipe requires more time and patience than others in the collection, but it pays off in a faux Negroni with the intricacy and dryness of its boozy sibling.

1 ounce **Gin Hydrosol** (recipe follows)
1 ounce **Sweet Vermouth Hydrosol** (recipe follows)
1/2 ounce plus 1 teaspoon **Terroirs du Liban bitter orange syrup** (available at terroirsduliban.com)
3/4 ounce **coconut water**
1 **orange twist**, for garnish

In a mixing glass, combine the gin hydrosol, vermouth hydrosol, bitter orange syrup, and coconut water. Fill with ice and stir briskly. Strain into a chilled rocks glass over a large ice cube. Squeeze the orange twist over the drink, rub it around the rim of the glass, then drop it in.

Makes 1 drink

GIN HYDROSOL

All of these dried herbs are available at Kalustyan's (foodsofnations.com). Don't be intimidated by the amount of ingredients. Outside of the time required to measure everything out, the cooking is done sous vide so you can leave the mixes alone while they simmer.

Makes about 20 ounces

1 liter (34 ounces) water
50 grams (1.7 ounces) dried juniper berries
10 grams (0.35 ounce) freshly grated lemon zest
10 grams (0.35 ounce) freshly grated orange zest
10 grams (0.35 ounce) freshly grated pink grapefruit zest
1 vanilla bean, split and seeds scraped
1 gram (0.04 ounce) dried lavender
1 gram (0.04 ounce) loose jasmine green tea
2 grams (0.07 ounce) sugar
Pinch of salt

Using an immersion circulator, heat a water bath to 131ºF (55ºC). Combine all the ingredients in a sous vide bag or mason jar. Vacuum seal and submerge in the water bath for 3 hours. Carefully remove the bag or jar, plunge it into an ice bath, and let cool to room temperature. Strain through cheesecloth into a large bowl. Transfer to a bottle, cover, and refrigerate for up to 2 weeks.

SWEET VERMOUTH HYDROSOL

Makes about 28 ounces

1 liter (34 ounces) non-alcoholic red wine
25 grams (0.9 ounce) dried wormwood (see Note)
5 grams (0.18 ounce) cassia bark
5 grams (0.18 ounce) dried orange peel
3 grams (0.1 ounce) dried lemon peel
3 grams (0.1 ounce) olive leaves
2 grams (0.07 ounce) dried licorice root
1 gram (0.04 ounce) dried ginger root
1 gram (0.04 ounce) whole cloves

Using an immersion circulator, heat a water bath to 131ºF (55ºC). Combine all the ingredients in a sous vide bag or mason jar. Vacuum seal and submerge in the water bath for 3 hours. Carefully remove the bag or jar, plunge it into an ice bath, and let cool to room temperature. Strain through cheesecloth into a large bowl. Transfer to a bottle, cover, and refrigerate for up to 2 weeks.

Note: Wormwood is a bitter herb that's long been used in the making of absinthe; used as a tea, wormwood can aid in digestion.

MANDY

Jose Alejandro Ibanez, *Employees Only, New York City*

A touch of vinegar goes a long way in giving no-proof drinks structure and longevity. While it's great to have a refreshing drink, sometimes it's key to have a drink that makes you slow down and savor it.

The Mandy starts with a citrus-forward kick, then morphs into a vegetal long drink with slightly bitter finish, courtesy of the fresh bell pepper juice and apple cider vinegar.

1 ounce fresh pink grapefruit juice
1/2 ounce yuzu juice
1/2 ounce fresh lime juice
1/2 ounce fresh yellow bell
    pepper juice
1/2 ounce agave nectar
1/4 ounce apple cider vinegar
Fever-Tree club soda,
    for topping, chilled
2 cucumber ribbons or wheels,
    for garnish
1 grapefruit twist, for garnish

In a cocktail shaker, combine the grapefruit juice, yuzu juice, lime juice, bell pepper juice, agave, and vinegar. Fill with ice and shake briskly. Strain into a chilled 12-ounce Collins glass filled with ice and top with club soda. Garnish with the cucumber. Squeeze the grapefruit twist over the drink, rub it around the rim of the glass, then discard.

Makes 1 drink

REX BANNER

William Wyatt, *Mister Paradise, New York City*

How do you fake umami and dark woody notes without alcohol? Create infusions using complex black teas and wood chips. In Will Wyatt's Rex Banner, you'll make a funky, very savory dark liquid that is unlike anything else in the no-proof space.

2¹/₂ ounces Mushroom Tea, chilled
   (recipe follows)
¹/₄ ounce pure maple syrup
1 orange twist, for garnish

In a mixing glass, combine the mushroom tea and maple syrup. Fill with ice and stir for about 15 seconds. Strain into a chilled 8-ounce rocks glass filled with ice. Squeeze the orange twist over the drink, rub it around the rim of the glass, then drop it in.

Makes 1 drink

MUSHROOM TEA

Makes about 16 ounces

1 quart filtered water
25 grams (0.88 ounce) loose
    lapsang souchong tea
10 grams (0.35 ounce) whole
    dried porcini mushrooms
15 grams (0.5 ounce) white oak
    wood chips

In a medium saucepan, bring the filtered water to a boil over high heat. Remove from the heat and immediately add the tea leaves. Let steep for 6 minutes. Strain through a fine-mesh strainer lined with cheesecloth into a large heatproof bowl; discard the tea leaves. Reserve the lined strainer. Return the brewed tea to the saucepan and bring to a boil over high heat. Reduce the heat to medium and simmer until the tea is reduced by half, about 20 minutes.

Remove from the heat and add the mushrooms. Let steep for 5 minutes, then strain through the reserved strainer into a large heatproof bowl. Discard the mushrooms. Set the mushroom tea aside to cool. Reserve the lined strainer.

Meanwhile, spread the oak chips in a single layer on the bottom of a small saucepan and lightly toast them with a kitchen torch until golden brown but not black. (If you don't have a torch, toast the chips in the saucepan over medium heat, without burning them, for 10 to 15 minutes.)

Transfer 2 cups of the mushroom tea to the canister of an iSi food whipper (see Note) along with the toasted oak chips. Charge the iSi canister with CO_2 according to the manufacturer's directions and let sit for 5 minutes. Release the gas from the canister (keeping the canister upright) and unscrew the lid. Strain the mushroom tea once more through the reserved strainer.

Transfer to an airtight container, cover, and refrigerate for up to 2 days.

Note: The iSi canister infuses the flavors in a matter of minutes; if you don't have an iSi canister, let the mixture sit overnight to infuse, then strain the liquid and discard the solids.

OLIVE HIGHBALL

Maxime Belfand, *Saxon + Parole, New York*

Savory and sparkly, Maxime Belfand's no-proof highball packs in the briny satisfaction of a dirty martini, and elongates the drink with a perfectly chilled tonic.

1 ounce Seedlip Garden 108 distilled non-alcoholic spirit (available at specialty stores and from Amazon)
1/2 ounce non-alcoholic sparkling brut wine, chilled
1/2 ounce Olive Shrub (recipe follows)
Large ice cube
1 (6.8-ounce) bottle Fever-Tree Mediterranean tonic water, chilled
1 black Cerignola olive and 1 red olive, pitted and skewered on a pick, for garnish
1 fresh bay leaf, for garnish

In a chilled 12-ounce highball glass, combine the Seedlip, sparkling wine, and shrub. Add a large ice cube and stir briskly. Slowly top with tonic water and garnish with the olives and bay leaf. Serve with the tonic bottle on the side.

Makes 1 drink

OLIVE SHRUB

Makes 3 ounces

25 grams (0.9 ounce) green Cerignola olives, pitted and sliced
50 grams (1.75 ounces) sugar
1 1/4 ounces apple cider vinegar
1/2 ounce water

In a medium bowl, combine the olives and sugar, cover, and let sit at room temperature for 72 hours, stirring occasionally.

Add the vinegar and water, stir to combine, then strain into an airtight container. Use right away or cover and refrigerate for up to 1 month.

THE RED PASSION

Salvatore Maggio, *The Franklin London—Starhotels Collezione, London*

The Red Passion's bright hue and luscious texture make it instantly memorable. The egg white gives this drink a foamy head, while the beets and raspberries deliver a slightly dry, earthy sip.

2 raspberries
1/2 teaspoon sugar
1³/4 ounces fresh beet juice
1³/4 ounces fresh red grape juice
1 large egg white
1 red grape, carved into a flower, for garnish (optional)

In a cocktail shaker, muddle the raspberries with the sugar. Add the beet juice, grape juice, and egg white; dry shake vigorously to emulsify. Fill with ice and shake again. Strain into a chilled 8-ounce coupe. Garnish with the grape.

Makes 1 drink

THE PERFECT COMBINATION

Salvatore Maggio, *The Franklin London–Starhotels Collezione, London*

The Perfect Combination is what its name suggests. Savory but also light, vegetal with a touch of dryness, this cocktail offers a lovely aftertaste and a satisfying froth.

5 cherry tomatoes
3 fresh basil leaves
1/2 teaspoon sugar
1³/4 ounces unfiltered apple juice
2 teaspoons fresh lemon juice
2 teaspoons tomato juice
2 teaspoons Bloody Mary mix
1 large egg white
1 fresh basil leaf, for garnish

In a cocktail shaker, muddle the tomatoes and 3 basil leaves with the sugar. Add the apple juice, lemon juice, tomato juice, Bloody Mary mix, and egg white and shake vigorously. Fill with ice and shake vigorously until the ice breaks up and the drink is frothy. Strain into a chilled 6-ounce coupe and garnish with the remaining basil leaf.

Makes 1 drink

UMAMI AND DADDY

William Wyatt, *Mister Paradise, New York City*

It's quite a feat to balance savory and delicate tones in a no-proof drink, but Will Wyatt pulls it off in this sophisticated vegetal martini-esque cocktail. The soft tomato and umami flavors are unmistakable, yet never overwhelming. When you want to show off, consider making this drink.

2 1/2 ounces **Tomato Water Dashi** (recipe follows)
1/2 ounce **chilled verjus blanc** (see Notes), **chilled**
1 **kinome leaf** (see Notes), for garnish

In a mixing glass, combine the dashi and verjus. Fill with ice and stir for about 25 seconds. Strain into a chilled 6-ounce Nick and Nora glass and garnish with the kinome leaf.

Makes 1 drink

Note: Verjus is the juice of unripe grapes. Because it's still a somewhat new category in the U.S., quality from new brands can range from excellent to funky. Look for verjus made by established wine companies, such as New York's Wölffer Estate.

Kinome leaf is the leaf of young sansho, a type of Japanese pepper. It's available at Japanese markets and chefs-garden.com.

TOMATO WATER DASHI

Consider this a version of slow food. There is not a lot of active cooking in making the dashi, but it does require several hours to let the mixture strain itself from a red pulpy mix into a clear yellow liquid. Your patience will be rewarded with an elegant, delicious base for a very special drink.

Makes about 24 ounces

10 medium beefsteak
    tomatoes, cored
1 fresh bay leaf
1 thyme sprig, leaves stripped
    and stem discarded
Kosher salt
1 (2x4-inch) piece kombu
    (dried kelp; available
    at Asian markets and
    health food stores and
    from Amazon)

Working in batches, combine the tomatoes, bay leaf, and thyme leaves in a blender. Blend on high speed until smooth (about 1 minute). Transfer each batch to a large pitcher or bowl. Strain through a fine-mesh sieve or conical strainer lined with 200-micron cheesecloth or a muslin cotton bag into a large bowl for 30 to 45 minutes, until the straining slows to about 1 second between drips. The strained tomato water should be light pink.

Transfer the sieve (with the tomato pulp still coating the cheesecloth) to another large bowl. Pour the strained pink tomato water through the sieve to strain again, this time in the refrigerator overnight. The liquid should be a pale golden yellow, but you will be able to see through it. Discard the pulp.

Measure the tomato water by volume and transfer to a saucepan. For every 1/2 ounce of tomato water, add 2 grams (0.07 ounce) kosher salt. Wipe the kombu with a damp cloth and add it to the saucepan.

Place the saucepan over low heat and gently warm, stirring slowly, until the salt dissolves and small bubbles begin to form on the surface of the dashi. Remove from the heat before it boils. Remove the kombu and discard. Let the dashi cool for 15 minutes.

Strain through a clean fine-mesh sieve or a cotton muslin bag into an airtight container. Cover and refrigerate for up to 2 days.

Note: Reusable muslin bags, such as those used to make nut milks, are very useful for straining this dashi.

SUPERDRY 2.0

Peder Schweigert, *Marvel Bar, Minneapolis*

Marvel Bar's Peder Schweigert swears by the Huilerie Beaujolaise calamansi vinegar that he recommends for this drink, which he created for Marvel's four-month dry drinks series. "This vinegar creates a really singular flavor in the drink and also makes for an incredible salad dressing should you not drink all of it," he says.

Very easy to put together, Superdry 2.0 hits you with a savory spark of vinegar, then unwinds into a summery citrus finish. This is a great example of a no-proof cocktail that stands on its own, without referencing traditional boozy recipes.

4 ounces club soda, such as Fever-Tree or London Essence, chilled
1/2 ounce fresh lemon juice
1/2 ounce Huilerie Beaujolaise calamansi vinegar (available at artisanalfoods.com)
1 dash salt tincture, such as Napa Valley Bitters fleur de sel tincture (available at NapaValleyBitters.com), or a small pinch of salt

Fill a chilled 12-ounce Collins glass with ice and add the club soda. Pour the lemon juice, vinegar, and salt tincture over the soda water, stirring gently to preserve the carbonation while mixing.

Makes 1 drink

N'ARTINI

Justin Lavenue, Sharon Yeung, and Caer Ferguson, *The Roosevelt Room, Austin*

A savory martini is one of the hardest no-proof drinks to get right. But look to the talents from Austin's Roosevelt Room to design a multilayered cold tea brew that replicates the herbaceous delights of a traditional London dry gin.

Verjus stands in for vermouth, and olive brine ties the drink together with a salty-savory bow in this slightly dirty yet high-stepping fresh martini.

4 ounces N'Artini Tea Batch
   (recipe follows)
¼ ounce verjus blanc (see Note)
¼ ounce Castelvetrano olive brine
1 lemon twist, for serving
2 olives, skewered on a pick,
   for garnish

In a mixing glass, combine the tea batch, verjus, and olive brine. Fill with ice and stir for 8 seconds, then strain into a chilled 8-ounce Nick and Nora glass. Squeeze the lemon twist over the drink, rub it around the rim of the glass, then discard. Garnish with the olives.

Makes 1 drink

Note: Verjus is the juice of unripe grapes. Because it's still a somewhat new category in the U.S., quality from new brands can range from excellent to funky. Look for verjus made by established wine companies, such as New York's Wölffer Estate.

N'ARTINI TEA BATCH

Makes about 20 ounces

2 cups boiling water
3/4 cup fresh Asian pear juice
    (from 2 to 3 Asian pears),
    filtered through coffee
    filters
3 ounces Seedlip Spice 94
    distilled non-alcoholic spirit
    (available at specialty stores
    and from Amazon)
12 juniper berry tea bags
10 whole cloves
3 star anise pods
2 fresh rosemary sprigs
2 fresh pine needle sprigs
1 gram (0.04 ounce) dried
    angelica root (available at
    foodsofnations.com)
2 fresh cucumber wheels
4 drops salt tincture, such as
    Napa Valley Bitters fleur
    de sel tincture (available at
    NapaValleyBitters.com),
    or a small pinch of salt
3/4 ounce vegetable glycerin
    (available at craft stores
    and from Amazon)
Peel from 2 small lemons
Peel from 2 small oranges

In a large heatproof bowl, combine all of the ingredients. Stir to combine. Cover, then let infuse in the refrigerator for 7 days. Strain through a fine-mesh chinois or sieve, then strain again through two coffee filters to remove any sediment. Transfer to airtight containers, cover, and refrigerate for up to 1 month.

TANGY & TROPICAL

PIRATE'S ANTHEM

Erick Castro, *Raised by Wolves, San Diego*

Tiki cocktails are a favorite style of drink due to their layers of flavors. In the Pirate's Anthem, from San Diego's award-winning Raised by Wolves, a few dashes of aromatic bitters and a surprise touch of maple syrup contribute to a no-proof tiki drink with depth.

1 ounce fresh orange juice
1 ounce pineapple juice
¾ ounce fresh lime juice
¾ ounce pure maple syrup
2 dashes Dale Degroff's pimento aromatic bitters (see Note)
4 dashes black walnut bitters, such as from Fee Brothers or Honest John (see Note)
Pebble ice
2 ounces Fever-Tree club soda, chilled
Pinch of freshly grated nutmeg, for garnish
1 fresh mint sprig, for garnish
1 star fruit slice, for garnish (optional)
1 pineapple leaf, for garnish (optional)

In a cocktail shaker, combine the orange juice, pineapple juice, lime juice, maple syrup, aromatic bitters, and black walnut bitters. Fill with pebble ice and shake well. Pour into a chilled 14- to 16-ounce tiki mug. Top with the club soda and more pebble ice. Sprinkle the drink with fresh nutmeg. Garnish with a mint sprig or with a star fruit slice and pineapple leaf.

Makes 1 drink

Note: Bitters have a trace amount of alcohol

KAMA'S ARROW

Tyson Buhler, *Death & Co, Denver*

Kama is the Hindu god of love, who shoots sensual flower arrows. Fizzy and fruity, this sprightly tropical drink has a lovely silky mouthfeel from the mango and cream of coconut, plus a lingering spiced finish. It might be love at first sip.

1 ounce fresh or frozen mango puree, such as Boiron (see Note)
1 ounce Vanilla Syrup (page 237)
½ ounce Coco López sweetened cream of coconut
½ ounce fresh lemon juice
2 dashes Scrappy's cardamom bitters (see Note)
La Croix coconut-flavored sparkling water, chilled, for topping
Crushed roasted pistachios, for garnish
Rose flower water, in an atomizer, for serving

In a cocktail shaker, combine the mango puree, vanilla syrup, cream of coconut, lemon juice, and bitters. Fill with ice and shake briskly. Strain into a chilled 12-ounce Collins glass, then top with the sparkling water and garnish with the pistachios. Spritz the rose flower water over the top of the glass.

Makes 1 drink

Note: Bitters have a trace amount of alcohol. Mango puree can be made at home in a food processor or purchased (Boiron makes excellent purees). The important thing is to use a puree with no added sugar.

STRANGE MAGIC

Tyson Buhler, *Death & Co, Denver*

A bright fruit-forward drink accented by baking spices, Tyson Buhler's Strange Magic balances citric tartness alongside vanilla and birch root beer–like notes. This cocktail makes a charming brunch companion.

The original bar version uses orange juice that's clarified via centrifuge; for home users, we've adapted the recipe to omit that step.

1¹/2 ounces fresh orange juice, strained through a fine-mesh sieve to remove the pulp
1¹/4 ounces verjus blanc, such as Wölffer Estate (see Note)
¹/2 ounce Vanilla Syrup (page 237)
6 drops birch extract (birch has notes of caramel with some spiciness; available from Amazon)
1 nasturtium leaf (available at specialty stores and chefs-garden.com), for garnish

In a mixing glass, combine the orange juice, verjus, syrup, and birch extract. Fill with ice and stir briskly. Strain into a chilled 6-ounce Nick and Nora glass and garnish with the nasturtium leaf.

Makes 1 drink

Note: Verjus is the juice of unripe grapes. Because it's still a somewhat new category in the U.S., quality from new brands can range from excellent to funky. Look for verjus made by established wine companies, such as New York's Wölffer Estate.

KING PALM

Tyson Buhler, *Death & Co, Denver*

Is there such a thing as a no-proof tropical martini? There is a small amount of prep that goes into making the kefir whey, but it pays off in a drink with silky textures, pockets of flavors, and a satisfying mouthfeel. Look for cinnamon and pineapple notes floating over a soft, savory finish.

1 ounce kefir whey (see Note)
2 ounces coconut water, chilled
1 teaspoon pineapple gum syrup (available at smallhandfoods.com, or make your own with Flavored Gomme (Gum) Syrup, page 238)
1 teaspoon Cinnamon Syrup (page 237)
1 lime wedge, for garnish

In a mixing glass, combine the whey, coconut water, pineapple syrup, and cinnamon syrup. Fill with ice and stir briskly. Strain into a chilled 6-ounce Nick and Nora glass. Garnish with the lime wedge on the rim of the glass.

Makes 1 drink

Note: Kefir whey is the liquid strained from kefir (a fermented milk product, similar to a thin yogurt). To make it, gently strain kefir through a fine-mesh sieve lined with four layers of cheesecloth. The first straining may take up to 1 hour. Take the strained whey, then filter again through clean cheesecloth, repeating until the whey runs clear. You will need about 8 ounces fresh kefir for just over 1½ ounces of kefir whey (you'll have a little extra left over in case of mistakes or for extra batches)

Don't waste the solid kefir; it's basically a very tangy, creamy yogurt. Chill and top with Mango Honey (page 200) for a delicious treat.

MELON MARKET SWIZZLE

Erick Castro, *Raised by Wolves, San Diego*

A successful no-proof drink delivers on texture, mouthfeel, and finish. In short, when well-constructed, the best non-alcoholic drinks don't make you wish for alcohol, but instead stand on their own. Consider the Melon Market Swizzle, which hosts a spectrum of flavors, ranging from herbaceous and minty to fruity and tangy. It might remind you of a traditional cocktail made with green Chartreuse.

Honeydew juice is the star in this drink. It doesn't have a long shelf life so use the freshest batch on hand.

12 to 15 fresh mint leaves
1 ounce Vanilla Syrup (page 237)
2 ounces fresh honeydew juice
1/2 ounce fresh lime juice
1/2 ounce Indian yogurt
    (or whole-milk Greek yogurt)
1 ounce Fever-Tree club soda, chilled
Pebble ice
1 fresh mint sprig, for garnish

In a mixing glass, lightly muddle the mint leaves with the vanilla syrup. Add the honeydew juice, lime juice, yogurt, and club soda. Fill with pebble ice and stir briskly. Pour into a chilled 13-ounce hurricane glass and garnish with the mint sprig.

Makes 1 drink

TROPICAL HARVEST

Natasha David, *Nitecap, New York*

Tiki, but make it no-proof. From its fragrant coconut aromas to its mango flourish, the compelling Tropical Harvest is sharp and herbaceous yet not overly sweet.

1½ ounces Seedlip Garden 108 distilled non-alcoholic spirit (available at specialty stores and from Amazon)
1 ounce Mango Honey
(recipe follows)
¾ ounce Coconut Cream
(recipe follows)
¼ ounce fresh lemon juice
Crushed ice (see page 16)
Toasted coconut, for garnish
Edible glitter, for garnish

In a cocktail shaker, combine the Seedlip, mango honey, coconut cream, and lemon juice. Fill with ice and shake briskly. Pour into a chilled 10-ounce double rocks glass. Mound crushed ice on top, snow cone–style. Top with the toasted coconut and sprinkle with edible glitter.

Makes 1 drink

MANGO HONEY

Makes about 8 ounces

3 tablespoons honey
1 tablespoon hot water
6 ounces fresh or frozen mango puree (see Note)

Combine the honey and hot water in a jar; stir until the honey dissolves. Stir in the mango puree. Cover and refrigerate for up to 2 weeks.

Notes: Mango puree can be made at home in a food processor or purchased (Boiron makes excellent purees). The important thing is to use a puree with no added sugar.

COCONUT CREAM

Makes about 20 ounces

1 (15-ounce) can Coco López sweetened cream of coconut
4½ ounces unsweetened coconut milk

Combine the cream of coconut and coconut milk in a medium bowl and whisk until incorporated. Transfer to an airtight container, cover, and refrigerate for up to 2 weeks.

GOLDEN OAT MILK

Natasha David and Jeremy Oertel, *Soho Diner, New York*

After making this drink, turmeric and vanilla might become one of your new favorite flavor combinations, if it's not already. Featuring a decadent swirl of creamy oat milk and a zap of ginger, Golden Oat Milk is memorable from the first sip to the last.

3 ounces oat milk, chilled
¾ ounce Vanilla Turmeric Syrup
  (recipe follows)
¼ ounce Ginger Syrup (page 238)
½ ounce fresh lemon juice
Crushed ice (see page 16)
1 dehydrated lemon wheel,
  for garnish (optional)
Dried oats, for garnish (optional)
1 ginger bud (available at Asian
  specialty markets), for garnish
  (optional)
1 vanilla bean pod, for garnish
  (optional)

In a cocktail shaker, combine the oat milk, both syrups, and lemon juice. Fill with ice and shake briskly. Strain into a chilled 10-ounce double rocks glass filled with crushed ice. Garnish with the lemon wheel and oats, or the ginger bud and vanilla bean for a more dramatic garnish.

Makes 1 drink

VANILLA TURMERIC SYRUP

Makes about 16 ounces

1 cup hot water
1 cup sugar
½ teaspoon pure vanilla
  extract
½ teaspoon ground turmeric

Combine the hot water, sugar, vanilla, and turmeric in a blender and blend until the sugar is dissolved. Pour into bottles, cover, and refrigerate for up to 2 weeks.

MANGO MANGO

Jim Kearns, *The Happiest Hour, New York*

Unmistakably tropical and vibrant, the Mango Mango starts with a crisp tang and softens as it melts. It's a perfect brunch companion.

2 ounces fresh or frozen mango
  puree (see Note)
1¹/2 ounces lime juice
1¹/2 ounces Simple Syrup (1:1)
  (page 236)
Chipotle salt (1 part chipotle powder
  mixed with 2 parts kosher salt)
Crushed ice (see page 16)

In a cocktail shaker, combine the mango puree, lime juice, simple syrup, and a pinch of chipotle salt. Fill with ice and shake briskly. Strain into a chilled 16-ounce double rocks glass, top with crushed ice (see Notes), and sprinkle the top with more chipotle salt.

Makes 1 drink

Note: Mango puree can be made at home in a food processor or purchased (Boiron makes excellent purees). The important thing is to use a puree with no added sugar.

THE GOOD OLD DAYS

Natasha David, *Nitecap, New York*

Like the Spice Road come to life, this cocktail is a heady mix of savory and sweet aromatics. Fresh pineapple notes provide the backdrop against an embroidery of vanilla, black tea, cinnamon, and cardamom accents. Add the seltzer a little at time so you don't drown out the delicate flavors in this exceptional drink.

1½ ounces Seedlip Spice 94 distilled non-alcoholic spirit (available at specialty stores and from Amazon)
½ ounce fresh lemon juice
½ ounce fresh pineapple juice
¼ ounce Vanilla Syrup (page 237)
¼ ounce Sous Vide Chai Syrup (recipe follows)
Seltzer, chilled for topping
1 pineapple wedge, for garnish

In a cocktail shaker, combine the Seedlip, lemon juice, pineapple juice, vanilla syrup, and chai syrup. Fill with ice and shake well; strain into a chilled 12-ounce Collins glass filled with ice, top with seltzer, and garnish with the pineapple wedge.

Makes 1 drink

SOUS VIDE CHAI SYRUP

A little bit of masala chai tea goes a long way in Natasha David's slow-cooked, deliciously fragrant syrup. An essential element of the Good Old Days cocktail, you'll keep returning to this syrup itself. Drop one or two spoonfuls in your tea or latte. Mornings will never be the same again.

Makes about 36 ounces

35 ounces Simple Syrup (1:1) (page 236)
5 grams (0.18 ounce) loose masala chai tea

Using an immersion circulator, heat a water bath to 135ºF (57ºC). Combine the simple syrup and chai in a mason jar. Cover tightly and submerge in the water bath for 2 hours. Carefully remove the jar, plunge it into an ice bath and let cool to room temperature. Strain the chai syrup through a fine-mesh sieve. Strain again through cheesecloth, if necessary. Return to the jar, cover, and refrigerate for up to 1 month.

Note: This recipe can be halved, however, I prefer to make the full amount and split the syrup between two airtight bottles. Keep one bottle in the fridge and another in the freezer until ready to use. Don't use glass for freezing syrups, and leave room at the top for the syrup to expand. Syrups kept in the freezer will stay fresh up to one year.

I AM NOT DRINKING TONIGHT

Alex Kratena, *Tayēr + Elementary, London*

Sea buckthorn berries are small and bright orange, with an intensely sour taste. Packed with three times the vitamin C as an orange, plus antioxidants and healthy fats, sea buckthorn (also called seaberry and sallow thorn) is popular across Europe, where it's mixed with other juices and sold as a "miracle food."

Sea buckthorn products are starting to emerge from U.S. health retailers (such as California-based Erbology, available from Amazon), but you can also find high-quality juices from European producers, such as Biokhaan, on Etsy and Amazon.

Scant ¾ ounce Everleaf non-alcoholic bittersweet aperitif (available at everleafdrinks.com and thewhiskyexchange.com)
1 ounce diluted sea buckthorn juice (see Notes)
½ ounce Minus 8 Maple Brix verjus (available at rareteacellar.com; see Notes)
2 teaspoons Rich Simple Syrup (2:1) (page 236)

In a cocktail shaker, combine the Everleaf, sea buckthorn juice, verjus, and simple syrup. Fill with ice and shake briskly. Strain into a chilled 12-ounce Collins glass filled with ice.

Makes 1 drink

Notes: If you're using 100 percent pure sea buckthorn juice, dilute it with 2 parts water (1 ounce juice plus 2 ounces water, for example). Sweeten to taste.

If you prefer a pre-mixed sea buckthorn juice, try Miracle Green Restore sea buckthorn juice (available from Amazon), which mixes sea buckthorn with green apple and other fruits. Don't dilute the Miracle sea buckthorn for this recipe.

MAI TAI TEA

Haera Shin Foley, *Momofuku Noodle Bar, New York*

Brisk but also tropical, you'll find an enticing swirl of Creamsicle-like sweetness, a hint of tartness from the blood orange juice, and a background dryness from the tea. The tea needs to be brewed strong to stand out against the citrus punch

3 ounces Taiwanese Black Tea, chilled (recipe follows)
1 ounce Calpico (Japanese yogurt-flavored soft drink; available at Asian markets and from Amazon), chilled
1 ounce pineapple puree
1 ounce mandarin orange puree
1 ounce fresh blood orange juice
1 dried blood orange wheel, for garnish
1 fresh mint sprig, for garnish
1 fortune cookie, for garnish

In a cocktail shaker, combine the tea, Calpico, pineapple puree, mandarin puree, and blood orange juice. Fill with ice and shake briskly. Strain into a chilled pint glass filled with ice. Garnish with the blood orange wheel, mint sprig, and fortune cookie.

Makes 1 drink

TAIWANESE BLACK TEA

Makes about 14 ounces

8 grams (0.28 ounce) loose Taiwanese black tea (available at Asian markets and from Amazon)
2 cups boiling water

In a medium heatproof bowl, combine the tea with the water; let steep for 8 to 10 minutes. Strain the tea into a heatproof jar and let cool to room temperature. Cover and refrigerate for up to 48 hours.

MARRAKECH EXPRESS

Mariena Mercer, *The Cosmopolitan of Las Vegas*

Mariena Mercer's drinks have turned Las Vegas on its head since the debut of the swish hotel The Cosmopolitan. Always inventive and surprising, she brings a culinary flair to all her drinks.

The Marrakech Express is a great example of her light touch, which ties citrus to a backbone of spices. The combination of rich coconut cream, fresh tropical flavors, and back notes of ginger and cardamom will remind you of a mango lassi.

2 ounces unsweetened coconut cream
1 ounce fresh or frozen mango puree (see Note)
1 ounce passion fruit puree
1/2 ounce calamansi puree
3/4 ounce Ginger Cardamom Syrup (recipe follows)
2 to 2 1/2 ounces ginger beer, chilled for topping
Crushed ice (see page 16)
1 fresh Thai basil sprig, for garnish
1 fresh passion fruit, halved, for garnish
1 fresh kiwi berry, for garnish
Pineapple, for garnish (optional)

In a cocktail shaker, combine the coconut cream with the mango, passion fruit, and calamansi fruit purees, and the ginger cardamom syrup. Fill with ice and shake briskly. Strain into a chilled pint glass. Add the ginger beer to your shaker, swirl it around, and then pour into the glass. Fill the glass with crushed ice, garnish with the basil, passion fruit, kiwi berry, pineapple, if using, and serve with a straw.

Makes 1 drink

Note: Mango puree can be made at home in a food processor or purchased (Boiron makes excellent purees). The important thing is to use a puree with no added sugar.

GINGER CARDAMOM SYRUP

Makes about 18 ounces

16 ounces Simple Syrup (1:1) (page 236)
2 tablespoons crushed green cardamom pods
7 1/2 ounces fresh ginger juice

Combine the simple syrup, cardamom pods, and ginger juice in a medium saucepan and bring to a boil. Reduce the heat and simmer for 20 minutes. Remove from the heat and let cool completely. Strain through a fine-mesh sieve into an airtight container. Cover and refrigerate for up to 1 month.

THE FAIR MATCH

Salvatore Maggio, The Franklin London—Starhotels Collezione, London

Kumquats, in season from November to March, pack an intense citrus zing into a tiny package. Showcased against fresh tropical juices and an unexpected hit of Christmas spices, this is an easy-drinking, sprightly concoction.

3 kumquats, plus 1 more
2 teaspoons gingerbread syrup (available at specialty stores and from Amazon)
3½ ounces passionfruit juice
1¾ ounces fresh pineapple juice
1 kumquat, sliced, for garnish

In a cocktail shaker, muddle 3 kumquats with the gingerbread syrup. Add the passion fruit juice and pineapple juice. Fill with ice and shake. Strain into a chilled 12-ounce Collins glass filled with ice. Slice the remaining kumquat and use it to garnish the drink.

Makes 1 drink

RICH &
DECADENT

VINTAGE RASPBERRY MILKSHAKE

Erick Castro, *Raised by Wolves, San Diego*

Erick Castro's vintage raspberry milkshake isn't a drink you can have every day, although you'll definitely want to. It's not cloyingly sweet, but it is silky and satisfying; it's a grown-up take on the classic dessert.

Gum syrup, a denser version of simple syrup, gives drinks body. You can purchase flavored gum syrup, or make your own by buying unflavored gum syrup and adding fresh juice to it, as needed.

2 ounces raspberry gum syrup (available at smallhandfoods.com, or make your own with Flavored Gomme (Gum) Syrup, page 238)
3 ounces heavy cream
1 large egg
Pinch of sea salt
2 ounces pebble ice
2 or 3 raspberries, skewered on a pick, for garnish

Combine the gum syrup, cream, egg, salt, and ice in a blender. Blend until smooth and pour into a chilled 12-ounce Collins glass. Garnish with the raspberries.

Makes 1 drink

PULUT HITAM

Nico de Soto, *Danico, Paris*

Nico de Soto's drinks are famous for taking inspiration from unexpected culinary corners. This cocktail is named after pulut hitam, a traditional Indonesian dessert that's a bit like a coconut-infused black rice porridge.

Silky and creamy, this drink is like a decadent Asian-inflected eggnog with caramelized banana and coconut notes and a gorgeous dry finish from the black rice. It's a fresh combination of flavors that pays off the effort of tracking down the ingredients.

1½ ounces Gekkeikan non-alcoholic sake (available at japancentre.com and markettokyo.ecwid.com; **see Note**)

1½ ounces Black Rice and Jackfruit Syrup (recipe follows)

1 ounce coconut milk

1 large egg

Takesumi Shio bamboo charcoal sea salt (available at MTCKitchen.com), for garnish

In a cocktail shaker, combine the sake, black rice syrup, coconut milk, and egg. Shake vigorously until frothy. Fill with ice, then shake vigorously again. Double strain (through a fine-mesh strainer, as well as the shaker's own strainer) into a chilled 8- to 10-ounce sake mug or rocks glass. Garnish with a dusting of sea salt.

Makes 1 drink

Note: Non-alcoholic sake is just starting to emerge as a category at many purveyors, so it's quick to sell out. With some luck and patience, you'll find it at online Japanese stores. Look for Gekkeikan's Alcohol Free (also called Laurel Crown Special-Free) in particular, which is made in the style of a dry sake; "amazake," another no-proof (or low-proof) product, is more available, but it's not the same thing.

BLACK RICE AND JACKFRUIT SYRUP

Originating in southern India and Malaysia, jackfruit is related to figs and mulberries, with a dense, chewy texture, a sharp ripe-banana-like aroma, and a flavor similar to lychee. Look for it at Asian markets.

If you buy jackfruit fresh, buy close to 1½ pounds to get enough puree. If you happen to end up with less puree than called for, just adapt the sugar and black rice mix so that it's always equal parts by weight.

Makes about 8 to 12 ounces

62.5 grams (2.2 ounces) uncooked black rice
250 grams (8.8 ounces) water
250 grams (8.8 ounces) fresh jackfruit puree (see Note)
250 grams (8.8 ounces) sugar

In a blender, combine the black rice and water. Blitz until blended, then strain through a fine-mesh sieve into an airtight container. The rice will absorb a lot of the water; you'll have to press on the mix to strain out as much water as you can, then discard the solids.

Weigh the black rice water and transfer it to a medium bowl. Add an equal weight of the jackfruit puree (e.g., 250 grams water to 250 grams puree); stir well to combine. Add an equal weight of sugar. Stir well or shake to combine.

Transfer the syrup to the airtight container, cover, and refrigerate for up to 2 weeks.

Note: To make jackfruit puree, separate the fleshy fruit from a 680-gram (1½ pound) jackfruit by hand, leaving aside the pulp and the big seeds. Blend the jackfruit flesh in a blender until smooth.

COFFEE COLD

Natasha David and Jeremy Oertel, *Soho Diner, New York*

With sweet cinnamon notes and rich coffee enveloped in a decadent froth, the Coffee Cold is a sophisticated take on the coffee & tonic, one of the bar world's favorite combinations. Don't have an espresso machine? Check out Jot Ultra Coffee, an intense coffee concentrate that allows you to mix up an espresso by adding hot water, no equipment needed.

1 ounce Seedlip Spice 94 distilled non-alcoholic spirit (available at specialty stores and from Amazon)
2 ounces espresso, chilled
¾ ounce Sous Vide Cinnamon Syrup (recipe follows)
2 ounces London Essence Co. tonic water, chilled
3 coffee beans, for garnish

In a cocktail shaker, combine the Seedlip, espresso, and cinnamon syrup. Fill with ice and shake well. Strain into a chilled 10-ounce double rocks glass filled with ice. Top with the tonic and garnish with the coffee beans.

Makes 1 drink

SOUS VIDE CINNAMON SYRUP

Cinnamon bark is one single layer from the cinnamon tree. It is high in essential oils, and is warmer, spicier, and sweeter than other parts of the plant. Cinnamon bark is preferred in this recipe, but cinnamon sticks can also be used. Drop a spoonful of this syrup into a fresh cup of Earl Grey tea to jazz up your mornings.

Makes about 32 ounces

30 ounces Simple Syrup (1:1) (page 236)
28 grams (1 ounce) cinnamon bark

Using an immersion circulator, heat a water bath to 135ºF (57ºC). Combine the simple syrup and cinnamon bark in a mason jar and seal. Submerge in the water bath for 2 hours.

Carefully remove the jar, plunge it into an ice bath and let cool completely. Strain the syrup through a fine-mesh sieve into a medium bowl. If necessary, strain again through a cheesecloth-lined fine-mesh sieve back into the jar. Cover and refrigerate for up to 1 month.

BLACKBERRY-LAVENDER FRENCH SODA

Daniel Sabo, *Lumière Brasserie at the Fairmont Century Plaza, Century City*

French sodas combine syrups with a touch of cream and cold fizzy waters. This drink isn't as thick as a milkshake but it does satisfy when you want something that's fruity as well as rich.

1½ ounces blackberry puree
1 ounce Lavender Syrup
   (recipe follows)
4 to 6 ounces Fever-Tree club soda, chilled
½ ounce half-and-half
3 blackberries skewered on a pick, for garnish

In a cocktail shaker, combine the blackberry puree and lavender syrup; add a few ice cubes and shake briefly. Add the club soda and strain into a chilled 12-ounce Collins glass filled with ice. Slowly add the half-and-half so that it creates an ombré effect. Garnish with the blackberries.

Makes 1 drink

Note: You can use a 10-ounce glass if you want less soda water. Adding too much water will mute the fresh berry flavors, so add a little bit at a time to suit your preference.

LAVENDER SYRUP

Makes 24 ounces

24 to 30 fresh lavender leaves (available at farmers' markets and in the plants section of grocery stores)
2 cups hot water
2 cups superfine sugar

In a medium bowl, combine the lavender with the hot water; let steep for about 15 minutes. Strain through a fine-mesh sieve into an airtight container; add the sugar and stir until it dissolves. Let cool completely, then cover and refrigerate for up to 2 weeks.

HIBISCUS CREAM PUFF

Erick Castro, *Raised by Wolves, San Diego*

Delightful. There are probably so many other words to describe Erick Castro's Hibiscus Cream Puff, but it's hard to get past the sheer joy this drink delivers. Inspired by the original milkshakes from turn-of-the-century soda parlors, this is a decadent treat that you'll savor until the end.

2 ounces Hibiscus Syrup
    (recipe follows)
3 ounces heavy cream
2 dashes Peychaud's Aromatic bitters
    (see Note)
Pinch of sea salt
2 ounces Fever-Tree club soda,
    chilled
2 ounces pebble ice
1 edible orchid
    (available at specialty stores
    and chefs-garden.com),
    for garnish

In a blender, combine the hibiscus syrup, cream, bitters, salt, 1 ounce of the club soda, and the ice. Blend until smooth. Stir in the remaining 1 ounce club soda, pour into a chilled 12-ounce soda fountain glass, and garnish with the orchid.

Makes 1 drink

Note: Bitters have a trace amount of alcohol.

HIBISCUS SYRUP

While hibiscus flowers are found in hibiscus teas, these teas will often contain flowers from other plants, which contribute different flavors.. To get pure hibiscus color and flavor in this syrup, look for dried whole flowers instead of tea.

Makes about 12 ounces

1 cup hot water,
    plus more as needed
2 ounces dried hibiscus flowers
1 cup sugar

In a medium heatproof bowl, combine the water and hibiscus and let steep for 30 minutes. Strain through a fine-mesh sieve into a measuring cup, pressing on the solids.

Add more hot water to yield 1 cup total, then add the sugar. Stir until the sugar is fully dissolved. Let cool completely, then cover and refrigerate. The syrup is best used within 10 days but can last up to 3 weeks.

AGUA DE AJONJOLÍ Y MANZANA FRESCA

José "Chuck" Rivera, *Jungle Bird, Puerto Rico*

You'll recognize all the ingredients in this recipe, yet the flavor profile in the drink will probably still catch you by surprise.

The drink features a homemade horchata, a spiced plant milk beverage, that leans heavily on sesame's fragrant note (*ajonjolí* is the Spanish word for sesame), and includes a miso syrup (see recipe below). When the extra-nutty agua de ajonjolí is introduced to manzana fresca, a stridently herbaceous green apple granita, the two melt into a savory, balanced drink that resists categories.

Pebble ice
3 ounces Agua de Ajonjolí, chilled
   (recipe follows)
1 ounce Manzana Fresca Ice
   (recipe follows)
1 freshly grated cinnamon stick,
   for serving
3 roasted, salted Marcona almonds,
   for garnish

Fill a chilled 12-ounce highball or sling glass about three-quarters of the way with pebble ice. Add the agua de ajonjolí.

Scrape the manzana fresca ice with a spoon to create granita-like icy shards, then mound it on top of the glass.

Freshly grate the cinnamon stick over the top, to taste, then garnish with the almonds. Serve with a straw.

Makes 1 drink

MISO SYRUP

Makes about 12 ounces

1 cup sugar
1 cup boiling water
1 tablespoon shiro (white)
   miso paste

Combine the sugar, boiling water, and miso in a medium heatproof bowl and stir until the sugar dissolves. Strain the syrup through cheesecloth or a fine-mesh sieve into an airtight container. Let cool completely, then cover and refrigerate for up to 1 week.

AGUA DE AJONJOLÍ

Makes about 28 ounces

1 cinnamon stick
1 star anise pod
2 whole cloves
2 allspice berries
2 cups ground untoasted
    sesame seeds (see Note)
6 cups water
14 grams (0.5 ounce)
    unsweetened coconut chips,
    toasted
10 grams (0.35 ounce)
    fresh lemongrass, chopped
5 grams (0.18 ounce) fresh
    ginger, peeled and chopped
6 ounces Miso Syrup
    (see page 226)

Heat a medium saucepan over low heat. Add the cinnamon, star anise, cloves, and allspice and heat, stirring, until lightly toasted. Add a splash of water and cook, stirring, until fragrant. Add the sesame seeds and cook, stirring, until golden, 1 to 2 minutes.

Add the water and heat to 270°F (132°C). Stir and bring to a boil over medium heat, about 5 minutes, then cook, stirring, for 5 minutes, more. Remove from the heat.

Add the coconut, lemongrass, and ginger; cover and let cool for about 15 minutes. Strain through a cheesecloth-lined fine-mesh sieve or muslin cotton bag overnight.

Add the miso syrup and stir to combine. Cover and refrigerate in an airtight container for up to 2 weeks.

Note: Grind the sesame seeds in a blender on high speed for 1 minute.

MANZANA FRESCA ICE

Makes about 14 ounces

16 ounces fresh cold-pressed
    green apple juice
50 grams (1.8 ounces) sugar
10 grams (0.35 ounce)
    fresh mint leaves
10 grams (0.35 ounce)
    fresh parsley leaves
10 grams (0.35 ounce)
    fresh cilantro leaves
5 grams (0.18 ounce)
    ascorbic acid
3 drops rose water
5 drops apple extract

Combine the apple juice, sugar, mint, parsley, cilantro, ascorbic acid, and rose water in a blender. Blend on high speed until smooth, about 1 minute. Strain through a fine-mesh sieve or cheesecloth into a large freezer-safe container. Add the apple extract and stir well to combine. Cover and freeze overnight, or until completely frozen. The mix will stay fresh in the freezer for up to two months.

BROOKLYN SPICE COFFEE

Elva Ramirez, *Brooklyn, New York*

A proper Irish coffee, with its hot liquid and cold cream float, is a truly magical thing. While I never turn down any offers of Irish coffee, the traditional heavy cream is too rich for my personal taste. Here's my zero-proof version of the classic drink, which doesn't lose anything in flavor but does make an important concession in terms of style: I skip the cream in favor of oat milk, resulting in a drink that's deliciously silky and nutty, albeit heretical to my Irish friends.

One of the reasons heavy cream floats on top of Irish coffee is its high fat content. In making a substitution of oat milk, you'll lose the fat, so it won't float in that perfect way. But by heating the oat milk, you can build froth and texture. You can pour or spoon the warm oat milk in slowly to try to get an ombré effect, but do note that you might not get the visual effect of its creamy counterpart. It won't look the same, but I prefer this particular combination of flavors. If you do want to go for that traditional Irish coffee serve, substitute very cold heavy cream for the oat milk.

4 ounces very hot strong
    brewed coffee
2 ounces Ritual Zero Proof
    whiskey alternative
    (available at ritualzeroproof.com
    and from Amazon)
½ ounce Cinnamon Syrup
    (page 237)
2 ounces Oatly oat milk or chilled
    heavy cream (see Notes)
Pinch of ground cinnamon,
    for garnish

In a 10-ounce Irish coffee mug, combine the coffee, whiskey alternative, and cinnamon syrup and stir to combine. In a small saucepan, heat the oat milk over medium-low heat, whisking constantly to build froth (see Notes). Once frothy, slowly spoon the oat milk into the glass. Sprinkle the cinnamon across the top.

Makes 1 drink

Notes: If using heavy whipping cream, keep it very chilled, then shake it in the container. Slowly pour the cold cream over a warmed spoon, so that the cream floats on top of the drink.

    You can use chilled Oatly instead of warming it in the saucepan if you prefer, but it tends to hold froth better when it is warm.

STRAWBERRY-PEPPERCORN FRENCH SODA

Daniel Sabo, *Lumière Brasserie at the Fairmont Century Plaza, Century City*

Silky and sweet, this French soda tastes best ice-cold, so be sure that both the club soda and the half-and-half are thoroughly chilled. With its float of cream and a vibrant strawberry flourish, the drink is charming without being cloying.

1½ ounces strawberry puree
1 ounce Pink Peppercorn Syrup
(recipe follows)
4 to 6 ounces Fever-Tree club soda, chilled
½ ounce half-and-half, chilled
Sliced strawberries, for garnish

In a cocktail shaker, combine the strawberry puree and peppercorn syrup; add a few ice cubes and shake briefly. Add the club soda, swirl in the shaker, then strain into a chilled 12-ounce Collins glass filled with ice (see Note). Slowly add the half-and-half so that it creates an ombré effect. Garnish with the sliced strawberries.

Makes 1 drink

Note: You can use a 10-ounce glass if you want less soda water. Adding too much water will mute the fresh berry flavors, so add a little bit at a time to suit your preference.

PINK PEPPERCORN SYRUP

Makes about 22 ounces

2 tablespoons cracked pink peppercorns
2 cups hot water
2 cups superfine sugar

In a liquid measuring cup, combine the peppercorns with the hot water; let steep for about 15 minutes. Strain through a fine-mesh sieve into an airtight container; add the sugar and stir until it dissolves. Let cool completely, then cover and refrigerate for up to 2 weeks.

INTERGALACTIC

Jason-Candid Knüsel, *American Bar at The Savoy, London*

Coffee, but make it stellar. The Intergalactic from London's revered American Bar amplifies the best parts of coffee by bringing nuttiness and spiced tropical notes to the foreground, and adding a surprise kiss of heat from a well-placed dash of hot chile pepper.

1 ounce high-quality cold brew coffee, such as Artemis or Stumptown, chilled
1 ounce Æcorn Aromatic non-alcoholic aperitif (available at aecorndrinks.com)
5 teaspoons Sous Vide Spiced Pineapple Syrup (recipe follows)
1/2 ounce fresh lime juice
2 drops hot pepper flavoring, such as Droplets Hot Chilli Pepper non-alcoholic flavoring (available at thewhiskyexchange.com) or Bittermens Hellfire Habanero shrub (available at bittermens.com and from Amazon; see Note)
1¾ ounces Fever-Tree club soda, chilled
Large ice cube

In a cocktail shaker, combine the coffee, Æcorn, pineapple syrup, lime juice, and hot pepper flavoring. Mix well with an immersion blender (or shake vigorously). Add the club soda, swirl in the shaker, then pour the drink into a chilled 12-ounce Collins glass over a large ice cube.

Makes 1 drink

Note: The Bittermens shrub has trace amounts of alcohol.

SOUS VIDE SPICED PINEAPPLE SYRUP

Makes about 8 ounces

4 ounces fresh pineapple
1 generous cup Rich Simple Syrup (2:1) (page 236)
25 grams (0.88 ounce) pink peppercorns
3 grams (0.1 ounce) whole cloves

Using an immersion circulator, heat a water bath to 140°F (60°C). Combine the pineapple, simple syrup, peppercorns, and cloves in a sous vide bag. Vacuum seal and submerge in the water bath 2 hours. Remove the bag and plunge it into an ice bath. Snip off one corner of the bag and strain the syrup into an airtight container. Cover and refrigerate for up to 2 weeks.

SYRUPS

SIMPLE SYRUP (1:1)

1 cup water
1 cup sugar

Bring the water to a simmer in a small saucepan, then remove from the heat. Add the sugar and stir until it dissolves. Let cool to room temperature, then store in an airtight container and refrigerate for up to 2 weeks.

Makes 12 ounces

RICH SIMPLE SYRUP (2:1)

1 cup water
2 cups superfine sugar

Bring the water to a simmer in a small saucepan, then remove from the heat. Add the sugar and stir until it dissolves. Let cool to room temperature, then store in an airtight container and refrigerate for up to 2 weeks.

Makes about 17 ounces

HONEY SYRUP (1:1)

1/2 cup hot water
1/2 cup honey

In a small saucepan, bring the water to a simmer. Remove from the heat, then add the honey and stir to combine. Let cool to room temperature, then store in an airtight container and refrigerate for up to 3 weeks.

Makes 8 ounces

HONEY SYRUP (2:1)

1/2 cup water
1 cup honey

In a small saucepan, bring the water to a simmer. Remove from the heat, add the honey, and stir to combine. Let cool to room temperature, then store in an airtight container and refrigerate for up to 3 weeks.

Makes 12 ounces

AGAVE SYRUP (1:1)

¼ cup water
¼ cup agave nectar

In a small saucepan, bring the water to a simmer. Remove from the heat, then add the agave nectar and stir to combine. Let cool to room temperature, then store in an airtight container and refrigerate for up to 2 weeks.

Makes about 4 ounces

AGAVE SYRUP (2:1)

¼ cup water
½ cup agave nectar

In a small saucepan, bring the water to a simmer. Remove from the heat, then add the agave nectar and stir to combine. Let cool to room temperature, then store in an airtight container and refrigerate for up to 2 weeks.

Makes about 6 ounces

VANILLA SYRUP

1 cup hot water
½ teaspoon pure vanilla paste
1 cup sugar

In a medium bowl, combine the hot water with the vanilla and stir well. Add the sugar and stir until the sugar is fully dissolved. Let cool to room temperature, then cover and refrigerate. The syrup is best used within 10 days, but will keep for up to 3 weeks.

Makes about 13 ounces

CINNAMON SYRUP

6 cinnamon sticks
2 cups sugar
1 cup hot water

In a medium bowl, combine the cinnamon sticks, sugar, and hot water. Stir to dissolve the sugar, then cover and let sit overnight at room temperature. Strain the syrup into an airtight container to remove any particles, then cover and refrigerate for up to 1 month.

Makes about 14 ounces

Note: See also the Sous Vide Cinnamon Syrup in the Coffee Cold recipe (page 221).

GINGER SYRUP

3 ounces Simple Syrup (1:1)
(page 236)
1 ounce fresh ginger juice,
strained

Combine the simple syrup and ginger juice in a small bowl. Stir to combine, then cover and refrigerate. The surup is best used within 2 weeks while the ginger flavor is potent but will keep for up to 1 month.

Makes about 4 ounces

Note: You can also buy a great ginger syrup from Morris Kitchen (morriskitchen.com).

FLAVORED GOMME (GUM) SYRUP

You can buy flavored gum syrups but I prefer to have a simple base that I add fruit to.

1 ounce Liber & Co. gum syrup
1 ounce fresh fruit puree,
such as strawberry

Combine the gum syrup and puree in a small bowl. Stir well to combine, then cover and refrigerate for up to 1 week.

Makes about 1³/4 ounces

CONTRIBUTORS

Giovanni Allario, *Le Syndicat Cocktail Club, Paris:* Following training in Italy and Spain, Giovanni is the head of acclaimed Parisian bar Le Syndicat, where a focus on French products is paired with a raucous party atmosphere.

Irving Araico, *Rufino, Mexico City:* A longtime Del Maguey Spirits bar ambassador, Irving is now at Mexico City's Rufino where he creates drinks that put a focus on fresh ingredients alongside traditional story and heritage.

Maxime Belfand, *Saxon + Parole, New York:* A French native who has worked in London and Mexico City, Maxime is now a proud New Yorker with a charming accent. Max is the bar manager at Manhattan's beloved Saxon + Parole, where the hospitality is as revered as the drinks.

Aidan Bowie, *The Aviary, New York:* From London's Dandylyan to New York's Aviary, Aidan has worked behind some of the world's most celebrated bars, and was named the U.K. finalist for Diageo's 2016 World Class competition. He's currently at the Dead Rabbit in New York.

Tyson Buhler, *Death & Co, Denver:* The former head bartender at Death & Co New York, Tyson is now beverage director for the Denver and Los Angeles Death & Cos. He's also the 2015 U.S. finalist in Diageo's World Class cocktail competition.

Erick Castro, *Raised by Wolves, San Diego:* Erick is co-owner of San Diego's Raised by Wolves. In 2019, Imbibe Magazine crowned Raised by Wolves the Cocktail Bar of the Year 2019 and Esquire included it as one of the Best Bars in America, 2019. Erick is behind the bar podcast, "Bartender at Large," and is a co-founder of Bartender's Weekend in San Diego.

Victoria Canty, *The Fat Radish, New York:* A former event producer and florist, Victoria created gorgeous, photogenic drinks at New York's Dante and The Fat Radish before joining the Lo Aperitifs team.

Ryan Chetiyawardana, *Lyaness, London:* Ryan, also known as Mr. Lyan, is one of the bar world's most highly decorated names. Among Ryan's many awards, you'll find *Imbibe Magazine*'s Personality of the

Decade, Drinks International's 2019 World's Most Influential Bar Personality, 2015 Tales of the Cocktail International Bartender of the Year, and 2009's Diageo top three Global Bartender of the Year. Ryan is behind Dandylan, named #1 World's Best Bar in 2018 by the World's 50 Top Bars, and the Tales of the Cocktail's 2017 World's Best Cocktail Bar. He currently has bar concepts in London, Washington D.C., and Amsterdam.

The Clumsies bar team, *The Clumsies, Athens, Greece:* What happens when two Diageo World Class finalists decide to open an all-day bar in a downtown Athens townhouse? Drinks magic and world class hospitality that catapults The Clumsies onto the lists of the world's best bars, and never comes off.

Natasha David, *Nitecap, Soho Diner, and Hotel Kinsley, New York:* As the co-owner of New York City's Nitecap, Natasha is one of the industry's most respected figures. She is Imbibe Magazine's 2020 Bartender of the Year, Eater's 2014 National Bartender of the Year, and a 2015 Star Chefs Rising Star; her drinks have been featured in multiple publications including the New York Times, Vogue, Nylon, and Wine & Spirits.

Nico de Soto, *Danico, Paris:* A truly international bartender, Nico has visited 87 countries and worked in 33 of them. He's the co-owner of Mace in NYC's East Village and Danico in Paris. Danico was a semi-finalist of Best New International Cocktail Bar in 2017 and a semi-finalist for Best International Restaurant Bar in 2018. In 2016, Nico was ranked as the 40th most influential French person in their thirties in French gastronomy, and the only bartender in the Top 50 of those recognized.

Meaghan Dorman, *Dear Irving and Raines Law Room, New York:* Meaghan Dorman is the bar director of New York City's Raines Law Room, Raines Law Room at the William, Dear Irving, and Dear Irving on Hudson. In 2015, Dear Irving was a Top 10 finalist for Tales of the Cocktail Best New American Cocktail Bar, and listed in *Esquire* magazine's 2015 Best Bars in America. Meaghan was *Imbibe Magazine's* 2016 Bartender of the Year.

Haera Shin Foley, *Momofuku Noodle Bar, New York:* Combining Japanese bar techniques with her native Korean heritage, Haera managed the drinks direction at Tao Group and Three Kings before landing at Momofuku, where she is spearheading innovations in seasonally driven bespoke draft cocktails.

Pippa Guy, *American Bar at The Savoy, London:* In 2017, Pippa became the first female senior bartender at the American Bar at The Savoy in over 100 years; in 2019, she was a finalist for Tales of the Cocktail's 2019's International Bartender of the Year. In early 2020, she joined the team at Crown Shy, one of Manhattan's most exciting venues.

Joseph Hall, *Satan's Whiskers, London:* Joseph was part of the Beaufort Bar at The Savoy when the team won Best International Hotel Bar in 2015. He left The Savoy to join London's acclaimed Satan's Whiskers, where he rose from junior bartender to head bartender. Under Joseph's direction, Satan's Whiskers was named British GQ's Best Bar of 2019 and #1 in the Top 50 Cocktail Bars.

Robert Hiddleston and Mia Johansson, *Bar Swift, London:* One of bartending's power couples, Mia and Bobby met at London's Milk & Honey and individually worked at several top bars, including the Dead Rabbit, Mark's Bar, and Callooh Callay. Bar Swift, opened in Soho in 2016, features a light-drenched aperitivo bar and a luxe, dark downstairs setting.

Jose Alejandro Ibanez, *Employees Only, New York:* A native of Colombia, Jose Alejandro ("Ale" to his friends) can be found at two of New York's busiest and most beloved bars, Employees Only and Macao where he works as bar manager (EO) and principal bartender (Macao).

Sam Johnson, *Death & Co, New York:* A Colorado native now living in New York, Sam worked at Pouring Ribbons, Clover Club, and Leyenda, before landing at Death & Co East Village, where he tends bar and teaches cocktail seminars. He is the 2017 International Sherry Cocktail Competition winner.

Alex Kratena, *Tayēr + Elementary, London:* As the former head bartender of London's Artesian bar, Alex and his team were recognized as the World's Best Bar at the World's 50 Best Bar Awards for four consecutive years. Named 2012's Best International Bartender by Tales of the Cocktail and *Imbibe Magazine*'s 2013 Bar Personality of the Year, Alex opened London's Tayēr + Elementary in 2019.

Jim Kearns, *The Happiest Hour, New York:* Following stints at Pegu Club and the NoMad Bar, Jim Kearns opened the Happiest Hour (and later Slowly Shirley) in Manhattan's West Village. Deploying a drink program featuring make-your-own mix-and-match cocktails with a range of bases, Happiest Hour is a favorite haunt of New Yorkers who come for the tasty drinks and stay for the playful vibes.

Jason-Candid Knüsel, *American Bar at The Savoy, London:* Jason is part of the acclaimed team at the American Bar at The Savoy, which has been serving since 1893. Given his work at one of the world's most famous bars, it's no surprise that Jason was part of Diageo's top 100 U.K. class of 2020.

Louis Lebaillif, *Little Red Door, Paris:* During his tenure as senior bartender at Paris's beloved Little Red Door, the bar was named #11, #33, and #36 on the World's 50 Top Bars list. Louis and his team explored a range of inventive techniques and developed conceptual menus that made the bar an industry darling. At the start of 2020, Louis joined Shofield's Bar in Manchester.

Jeremy Le Blanche, *queensyard NYC:* With experience at top bars in Switzerland, France, and London, Jeremy brings an international, inventive flair to his drinks. As the debut beverage director of New York's queensyard, his drinks are known for culinary inspiration and refined presentation.

Justin Lavenue, Sharon Yeung, and Caer Ferguson, *The Roosevelt Room, Austin:* Justin won Bombay Sapphire's Most Imaginative Bartender 2015 competition in Las Vegas, and was named one of *Food & Wine* magazine's Best New Mixologists of 2015. He opened The Roosevelt Room in 2015. Sharon Yeung is the head bartender at The Roosevelt Room. Caer Ferguson is a bartender at The Roosevelt Room, and the bar manager at The Eleanor, its adjacent event venue.

Salvatore Maggio, *The Franklin London—Starhotels Collezione, London:* With nearly three decades of experience, Salvatore has worked at several of London's top bars including The Ritz London, the St. James Hotel, and the private members-only Morton's Club in Mayfair. Following a stint as the head bartender at The Franklin Hotel, he took on the bar manager position at London's luxury Kensington Hotel.

Paul Mathew, *Everleaf Drinks, London:* Paul is a conservation biologist and bartender with over two decades of experience. He launched Everleaf, a non-alcoholic aperitif, in January 2019 to meet demand from his guests for great non-alcoholic options with all the flavor, complexity, and texture of the best spirits in the world.

Lynnette Marrero, *Llama Inn, New York:* Lynnette is the bar director at the Brooklyn hotspot Llama Inn and Llama San, which received a glowing three-star review from the *New York Times*. A former Diageo rum brand ambassador, she's also the national brand mixologist for Perrier Sparkling Water and San Pellegrino Sparkling Fruit Beverages. She was named Wine Enthusiast's Mixologist of the Year in 2016 and is the co-founder of Speed Rack, the female-led bartending philanthropy.

Mariena Mercer, *The Cosmopolitan of Las Vegas:* Specializing in molecular mixology, inventive garnishes, and tequila, Las Vegas native Mariena Mercer was behind a new wave of cocktail culture as the Cosmopolitan's chef mixologist. She oversaw 21 different menus at the resort, and in 2018 alone, drink sales topped $75 million. One of her drinks minted over $8.4 million in revenue, despite not being advertised on any menu.

Jeremy Oertel, *Soho Diner and Hotel Kinsley, New York:* With over 15 years of experience, Jeremy has worked several top New York bars including Death & Co, Dram, and Donna. His drinks have been featured in the *Wall Street Journal, New York Times, Food & Wine, Time Out New York, New York* magazine, *Huffington Post, New Yorker,* among others.

David Paz, *Xaman, Mexico City:* From Mexico to Paris, David Paz brings a culinary, locavore flair to his drinks. With experience at Mexico City's lauded Licoria Limantour and Xaman, David was most recently based in Paris, working at La Mezcaleria and Bonhomie.

Sean Quinn, *Death & Co, Denver:* Sean Quinn brings a playful spirit to his drinks, as evidenced by his charming Child's Play, which references the nostalgia-inducing notes of vanilla, orange, and caramel.

José "Chuck" Rivera, *Jungle Bird, Puerto Rico:* As the former head bartender at Jose Andres's Mini-bar/Barmini, Chuck worked with a team that was nominated for the James Beard Outstanding Bar Program awards in 2015 and 2016. Currently based in Puerto Rico, Chuck is the R&D director and partner in Colectivo Ícaro, which owns acclaimed venues La Factoría and Jungle Bird.

Eamon Rockey, *Listen Bar and Betony, New York:* Following a career at Eleven Madison Park and Atera, Eamon worked alongside chef Bryce Shuman at Manhattan's highly lauded Betony, where his beverage program is credited with bringing elevated milk punches back into fashion. In 2018, he launched Rockey's, a bottled milk punch product. He is also the director of beverage studies at the Institute of Culinary Education, launching the program in early 2020.

Daniel Sabo, *Lumière Brasserie at the Fairmont Century Plaza, Century City:* Dan was tapped to mastermind the bar direction at the Ace Hotel DTLA and later assisted with Ace Hotel openings in Pittsburgh and New Orleans, before moving on to oversee food and beverage direction at nine of L.A.'s boutique Palisociety Hotels. He's currently the food and beverage director at the Fairmont Century Plaza.

Peder Schweigert, *Marvel Bar, Minneapolis:* A graduate of the French Culinary Institute, Peder is a former culinary producer on *Top Chef* season 5 and also worked in the kitchen of Chicago's highly lauded Alinea. The chef turned bartender lent his culinary expertise to the inventive drinks at Minneapolis's acclaimed Marvel Bar.

Aaron Michael Siak, *Bibo Ergo Sum, Los Angeles:* A former licensed real estate broker and certified public accountant, Aaron is a rising star in bartending, working at L.A.'s The Walker Inn and accomplice bar, before tackling the general manager role at drinks palace Bibo Ergo Sum.

Devon Tarby, *Bibo Ergo Sum, Los Angeles:* Devon is a partner at Proprietors LLC, a full-service hospitality firm that owns, operates, and consults on a myriad of projects within the beverage sphere, including the Death & Co properties. Over the last five years, Devon and her partners have consulted on over two dozen bar openings and beverage programs both in the U.S. and abroad. In 2014, Devon was named Star Chefs Rising Star Bartender for her work on the opening menu at Los Angeles's Honeycut.

Camille Vidal, *La Maison Wellness, London:* As the former global ambassador for St-Germain, for which she was named Tales of the Cocktail 2017 Best International Brand Ambassador, Camille is a leading voice in the drinks industry, particularly in the no- and low- drink category. Now the founder of the mindful drinking brand and creative consultancy La Maison Wellness, she is focused on guiding brands and organizations to elevate wellbeing in hospitality.

Christine Wiseman, *Broken Shaker at the Freehand, Los Angeles:* A bar veteran who started out as a chef, Christine brings star-quality charisma and inventiveness everywhere she works. She was a semi-finalist for American Bartender of the Year in 2018 and 2019, and her drinks have been featured in *Food & Wine, Thrillist National, GQ,* and *Punch,* among others.

William Wyatt, *Mister Paradise, New York:* Following stints at New York's Experimental Cocktail Club, the NoMad Bar, and Mace, Will opened his own bar, Mister Paradise, in New York's East Village where inventive sophisticated drinks are served in a cheery, often exuberant, atmosphere.

ENDNOTES

INTRODUCTION

1 Global beer volume: AB-InBev, Sept. 2018. https://www.ab-inbev.com/news-media/news-stories/How-we-are-changing-the-way-people-think-about-Smart-Drinking.html

2 Non-alcoholic sales: Arthur, Rachel. "Carlsberg: 'We are seeing a significant increase in alcohol-free," BeverageDaily.com. Feb. 7, 2019.

3 Up 35 percent: Hancock, Edith. "This Is How Many People Are Planning To Give Up Alcohol for Dry January 2019," *The Drinks Business*. Dec. 2018.

4 Teetotalism has increased: Office for National Statistics, Adult Drinking Habits in Great Britain: 2017. https://www.ons.gov.uk/peoplepopulationandcommunity/healthandsocialcare/drugusealcoholandsmoking/bulletins/opinionsandlifestylesurveyadultdrinkinghabitsingreatbritain/latest

5 Reported they were teetotalers: Donnelly, Laura. "Millennials shunning alcohol as getting drunk is no longer cool," The Telegraph. Oct. 2018.

A BRIEF HISTORY OF TEMPERANCE: COLONIAL ERA TO EIGHTEENTH CENTURY

6 Beer kept away signs of scurvy: Cheever, Susan. *Drinking In America*. Hachette Book Group. New York. 2015. Pg. 21

7 Set up by the pilgrims: Ibid. Pg. 25

8 "sober lifestyle and a healthy diet": Gately, Ian. *Drink: A Cultural History of America*. Penguin Group. New York. 2008. Pg 121.

9 Settler Thomas Studley wrote: Tyler, Lyon Gardiner. Narratives of Early Virginia, 1606—1625. *Scribner's Sons*. New York. 1907. Pg 127.

10 Virginia Governor George Percy: Ibid. pg 22

11 "wild vomits": Grizzard, Frank and D. Boyd Smith. *Jamestown Colony: A Political, Social, and Cultural*

History. ABC-CLIO. Santa Barbara. 2007

12 Waterborne disease": Earle, Carville. Geographical Inquiry and American Historical Problems. Stanford University Press. Stanford. 1992

13 Cannibalism during the winter of 1609: Stromberg, Joseph. *Smithsonian Magazine.* April 2013. https://www.smithsonianmag.com/history/starving-settlers-in-jamestown-colony-resorted-to-cannibalism-46000815/

14 "no choice, drank water": Chappelle, Frank. Wellsprings, A Natural History of Bottled Spring Waters. Rutgers University Press. New Brunswick. 2005. Pg. 102.

15 And then again after dinner: Rorabaugh, W.J. The Alcoholic Republic: An American Tradition. Pg 19.

16 Came in at 1 percent alcohol: Ibid, Pg 9.

17 "twenty-shilling fine": Drinking in America. Pg 26.

18 "nine million women": Drink, pg 231.

19 Fuddles the head": Ibid.

20 By 1850: The Alcoholic Republic. Pg 41.

21 Naturally effervescent water: Wellsprings, pg. 111.

22 "gives hilarity": *The Enquirer.* Richmond, Va. May 31, 1811.

23 Published in 1881: Winskill, P.T. The comprehensive history of the rise and progress of the temperance reformation: from the earliest period to September 1881.

24 the use of ardent spirits: Ibid, pg. 10.

25 "other drinking instrument whatsoever": Ibid. pg 6.

A BRIEF HISTORY OF TEMPERANCE: LATE 1800S TO PROHIBITION

26 An entire article was devoted: "Where The Bill Was Signed," *The Journal,* March 24, 1896.

27 "In the East Side district": "Drinks In Plenty, And Few Arrests," *The Journal,* May 11, 1896.

28 "To get a drink": "Fierce Fight, After Much Beer In Coney," *The Journal,* May 18, 1896.

29 1,200 egg phosphates: White, April. "When the Temperance Movement Opened Saloons." JStor Daily. July 13, 2017.

30 "One downtown drug store": "Cool Things To Drink," *The Journal,* July 19, 1896.

31 Soda sales added up: "Who Put the Fizz in Soda Water?", *The New York Times.* Sept. 14, 1913.

32 "Coffee is increasing": "Coffee-Drunken New York," The New York Times Magazine, Sept. 16, 1923.

33 "the aproned bartender": "Episcopal Church to Run Places Called 'Saloons'," *New York Tribune,* Oct. 31, 1919.

THE MOCKTAIL ERA

34 "the effects of alcohol": Marks Jr., Edward. "The Drys Crusade Again But with New Tactics," *The New York Times.* Oct. 25, 1936.

35 "Smirnoff bottle filled with water": "That's a Drink? Nope, It's a Mocktail," *The Chicago Tribune,* published in the Hartford Courant. Aug. 10, 1978.

36 Curbing drunken driving: Associated Press. "Washington mocktail party opens campaign on drunk driving," *Chicago Tribune.* Dec. 14, 1984

37 1985 New Year's Eve op-ed: Heinzmann, Barbara. "Cheers to New Year's Drinking—Without Alcohol." *Orlando Sentinel.* Dec.31, 1985.

DRY JANUARY AND THE RISE OF NEW MODERATION

38 December 2005: Stein, Jeannine. "Tough? Try not drinking for a month; Skipping alcohol boosts workouts, the instructor vowed. But few counted on the peer pressure." *Los Angeles Times.* Dec, 12, 2005.

39 Post-revolutionary America: Rorabaugh, pg. 151.

40 Alcohol Change UK: "Charity issues drinkers with challenge to have a 'dry' January." *The Western Mail.* Nov. 12, 2012.

41 At least 1637: Winskill, pg. 5.

42 Market research firm Mintel: Bryant, Caleb. "Why Dry January is more popular than ever." Mintel. com. Jan. 13, 2020. https://www.mintel.com/blog/drink-market-news/why-dry-january-is-more-popular-than-ever

43 According to researchers: Ford, Anna. "How 'Dry January' is the secret to better sleep, saving money and losing weight," University of Sussex. Jan. 2, 2019.

44 In 2018, The Lancet: GBD Alcohol Collaborators. "Alcohol Use and Burden for 195 Countries and Territories: 1990–2016," *The Lancet.* Aug. 23, 108.

45 Risk for health issues: Bakalar, Nicolas. "How Much Alcohol Is Say to Drink? None, Say These Researchers." *The New York Times.* Aug. 27, 2018.

46 Roni Caryn. "Major Study of Drinking Will Be Shut Down," *The New York Times,* June 15, 2018.

47 liquor brands to fund the trial: Rabin, Roni Caryn. "It Was Supposed to Be an Unbiased Study of Drinking. They Wanted to Call It 'Cheers.'" *The New York Times,* June 18, 2018

48 Categorized as alcohol-related: White, Aaron et al. "Using Death Certificates to Explore Changes in Alcohol-Related Mortality in the United States, 1999 to 2017," Alcoholism Clinical and Experimental Research. Jan 2020.

49 "a problem with drinking": Williams, Alex. "The New Sobriety." *The New York Times Magazine.* June 16, 2019.

50 The chef was said: Samuel, Henry. "Forget Dry January: French superchef urges diners to drink 'by the bottle rather than the glass." *The Telegraph Online,* Jan. 15, 2020.

51 "struggling breweries and pubs": Torre, Berny. "Brit brewers demand an end to' Dry January' campaign as pubs suffer," *The Daily Star.* Nov. 22, 2019

THE AGE OF THE NO-PROOF COCKTAIL

52 About the no-proof concept: Passy, Charles. "A Speakeasy Without Spirits," *The Wall Street Journal.* Oct. 23, 2018.

INDEX